ZIMBABWE:
BEYOND ROBERT MUGABE

*

Essays, Non Fictions and Letters

*

Tendai Rinos Mwanaka

Mwanaka Media and Publishing Pvt Ltd,
Chitungwiza Zimbabwe

*

Creativity, Wisdom and Beauty

i

Publisher: *Mmap*

Mwanaka Media and Publishing Pvt Ltd

24 Svosve Road, Zengeza 1

Chitungwiza Zimbabwe

mwanaka@yahoo.com

mwanaka13@gmail.com

https://www.mmapublishing.org

www.africanbookscollective.com/publishers/mwanaka-media-and-publishing

https://facebook.com/MwanakaMediaAndPublishing/

Distributed in and outside N. America by African Books Collective

orders@africanbookscollective.com

www.africanbookscollective.com

ISBN: 978-1-77924-320-1

EAN: 9781779243201

DISCLAIMER

All views expressed in this publication are those of the author and do not
necessarily reflect the views of *Mmap*.

ii

Table of Contents

Introduction

I wrote letters to Robert Mugabe, Constantine Chiwenga, Morgan Tsvangirai, The Zimbabweans, Emerson Mnangagwa, Nelson Chamisa, The Police, and in between them I infused these letters with deeply literary and psychoanalytic essays on what motivated the players in Zimbabwe to do what they did or are doing. I want to use this nonfiction literary form, the letter writing form, to protest against Robert Mugabe and the Mugabeism, our ever-present jailer! The mistake we can now make is to think it's over just because Mugabe eventually left. The system is still the same that has been used by Mugabe to subject the country under his vicious thump. Until we have changed the whole system, there is no reason we should start to have faith with just a change of faces in the ZANU-PF.

I started writing these letters to protest against Mugabe's continuing clinging to power in 2017 but I have expanded this to include a lot other issues, issues to do with the system, culture, church etc... Zimbabwe will move towards a better multiparty democracy if there is change in thinking in these very important facets shaping Zimbabwe. Each letter will tackle each of the important issues at the heart of *Zimbabwe: Beyond Robert Mugabe;* constitutionalism and rule of law, change and devolution of government, developmental agenda, and freedom of expression and association. Let's be confident that the religion of resistance will always triumph over the technology of repression. This act of collecting them into a book is equivalent to posting them; I am posting these letters into the wind, and let the wind carry forward my messages to the world over. I know that even a rock dreams that it was a mountain, that's why we have stone heads on top of mountains. Instead of reaching outward to change the world and scare off, I am looking inward to experience it, to change myself and others, to create authentic lasting power.

I just write down what was in my heart as if I was just writing it to myself, or just reading the situation to myself. When we create authentic power again and again, we become authentically connected and powerful. This exercise is also an opportunity for each of us to process the anger and pain we have against Robert Mugabe. The streets are ready for us. I will use this process to heal and find peace with myself again. It is a chance to love ourselves again, and find faith in this country we call home, which Mugabe has made his playground. *Trust the grate's fire to again allow songs in Zimbabwean homes!*

Silence

For some years I have been a great desert of silence, green silence, screaming silence, painful silence; building extensions into my own heart, making many divisions (departments, ministries and organisations) of silence. I had been logging silence like a seed into the embryo of silence I had in every of those divisions of silence my heart. My heart had been galloping with me, filling itself up with silence. No one was astriding it. Read this book, perhaps you will figure out how the plot will unfold, or fold back into itself? Perhaps this silence in my heart will put present's fear of the past, and of the future, out of my heart.

But I still have this unwavering idea that it's up to me, not anyone else, for me to free myself from this harsh and demanding bandage of silence. This silence simply has to oblige me at some point. Of course, this silence has been very calculating, in buying me into submissiveness, into quietness, too. Now the words inside my heart are cursing themselves without even saying a single thought. So, this goes on and on for some long minutes. I have happened upon this deep silence. This is the silence: of the silence of inner landscapes. It is eternal silence. How much can I now be able to let you see?

I start to measure silence for you. Frame it well inside the walls of my heart. No mouth opens in my heart, no window opens, nothing inside my heart is removed, and nothing is added inside me. Everything is the voice of silence; my silences are many silenced words. The silence in

1

my heart is like pins and needles- ice shards in my heart. I am a silent being. I am not becoming. The inside of my heart is now the most silent place in my whole being. Only I can decide to continue sharing it with you.

There is no speech flowing through these divisions in my heart, but only murmurs of un-speech. The murmurs are so soft and seem to take me inside my heart by hand. Yet, they do not silence the borders of these divisions of silence, in my heart. These are the borders that have separated me from myself. I am not here. I am not there. I am entrapped within these multiple borders of silences. Whilst the silence is crowding upon me, crowds and crowds of silence, the language of silence becomes the language commanding me to pour out my soul, until I gather some sound in my heart. So that the silence inside my heart started commanding me, *speak, speak, speak...* This speaking is a major ceremony among the living, but there are still gaps inside my heart that even these sweetened words couldn't bridge, the empty gaps that should have filled up my mind. They are many, many silences, in these gaps; the silence as of the thunderclaps. They are a few other sounds in this universe that threatens silence like thunderclaps.

Using these scented snippets that have already escaped from me; a voice has come to me: it is a voice capable of the greatest tenderness and wander from a hard suffered unsparing awareness of displacement and loss and; to live in the danger again! This voice, like the silence, is a major ceremony among the living too, the silence in the voice is part of talking and to talk is to risk. What?

The silence of an unknown prisoner, abandoned to humiliations, is enough to open me up to some kind of a talk. I hope I won't forget the silence whilst talking and to transmit to it so that I can manage to resound to my story. I find something irresistible and begin to crawl towards it. I find my tongue in writing these words, these feelings, in the shades of grey; in writing of the tell-tale scars and lines, in the telling of the silences of my life. I am sorry and regretful that this is all that is coming out of me, at this moment. There are no barriers anymore in me but the silence that I have always carried with me, for all of my life. It thrusts everything aside. It's not so much shadows that I now hold.

My mouth, void of teeth, is a gapping crater. The alleyways are dark, wooden doors opening and closing with this telling. It seems I have been making paths inside me just as they have been paths outside of me. Complex writings- threatening- it is the idea of never being spoken to again in life. Yet, I am talking. It is an ultimate human punishment, not to be talked to, exclusion..., nonexistence, I know that. The illegible letters are harsh, but the meanings remain unknown and lost to anything; or to anyone, until one has had to go through those same silences. Some silences are irretrievable... the silences of broken things, betrayal, death. These silences haunt us. They are no answers, no replies and in these silences something usually arrives.

One night, one good night ringed out to me. I found my thoughts totally blocked, totally jammed with memories and feelings of the past. The noise and chaos caused was so bad. The nouns popped up again and again, their instructions specific, but swarming with words, with people, with people ideas. My heart was beginning to choke; calling this night away. My heart was the echo of nothing. Neither my heart's cracked stones nor my heart's sharp turns could help me lift this decree from me. My language became deaf.

When something like that happens, you retreat into a place within yourself that no one else can reach. What was once a sanctuary becomes a prison? That meant your heart couldn't recognise how and when the external time had been passing. You would go to the bathroom at one point and look deeper into your own eyes in the mirror, but you are too troubled to really figure out what question you were hoping to answer. You also know, you have to lose yourself before you could find someone else who looks back in the mirror, even if it is you in the mirror. You couldn't also realise that the inner time, in your heart, had all along been stationary, creating these difficulties of time adjustments!

Part of me had been growing yet another part of me had been refusing to grow. Some of the divisions of my heart had been growing yet some divisions had not been growing. That was not the entity I had owned all those years of silence. That division of my heart that allows the sense of belonging was also flooded with too many thoughts, with too many silences. It consisted basically of an immense knot of roads of silences, north and south, east and west, overlapping silences too. My heart had not been missing the words but it had been dangerously adding unexpected vibes, too; less concrete of their old speech. My heart had not known that I had returned to my heart.

I tried to lubricate every road with words. I also tried to thrust my hands into the soft mulch of these familiar words, and that's the mistake that I made. It was the wrong type of lubricant. One of the words did nothing at all but daubed the filigree of my wounds. All thoughts and decisions became mute. I got completely confused, dumb, numb, clam. Each word didn't have its own specified and compartmentalised function. Ideas and thoughts that had unhinged from the words were going both northwards and southwards, others were completely running berserk, and some derailed off the tracks, creating obstructions and blocking the smooth flow in these roads. It was total chaos. It took me a lot of time to calm myself. Confronting the failure of words and silence to co-exist together is like an idle attempt to re-make reality out of trauma.

But now, I have a task; to do a meticulous clearing of the residues of thoughts and ideas, words, and torn fragments of silences. I have to comb even my hair for silence, and for dried and broken fragments of speech: collecting all these for burning. These are my opinions, thoughts and feelings: sacrifice, scrapping. Baskets have to be filled up with forgotten ideas, words, thoughts... and broken silences too, by this visit of speech before another silence. Confidence is the evidence of my healing so I have taken a vow to break the silence against this angry slowness of my mind.

The Portrait Of...

When I recall of my early childhood years, way back in the 1970s, Mugabe was already in my world of things. Then, he was a saviour, trying to liberate us from the oppressive yoke of the colonialists. At home, he was always on the radio. We didn't have a television set. I didn't know him, his portrait, his pictures... I had never seen him, but in my mind, I had created an image of a huge soldier, so dashing, confident and strong. When I started going to school in the 80s, it's when I saw his pictures, for the first time. His pictures were all over the school building walls, all over shops, all over public places. He had these brooding good looks and he filled the portraitures with his light; a dark light. He was well respected by people, and some even thought he was their god. He was made to be that by our elders who worshiped him.

In those early years the idea that someone could be worshipped didn't exist in my world. I wasn't even a believer. I didn't believe in anything, other than the availability of my family and that playing was a given, and was the greatest thing that could ever happen to a person. So I liked it when we roved in the fields and meadowlands, playing all sorts of games. In that world, he didn't exist for me. He had no way to intrude upon me. Back then, I didn't think of him much for he wasn't a partner or an opposing figure in our games. Yet when we were in public places he was this huge person who was always watching us, spying on our privacy, telling us he knows everything that we think, want to do, our names, our futures. It seems he was telling us, on his elevated stand on the walls, that we would never aspire to be like him, that we have to stay below him, that he was the best there was in our country, in our world, he was our God. I have enthused before about how the Gods love elevated high places. How we raise them into elevated places. And we felt that he would always be the measure by which everyone else in the country will be measured by. Back then, there were not many jokes or jibes made of those pictures. Somehow those pictures were sacred, so he didn't have to be derided.

We were little so we didn't care that much unless when we were forced to give allegiances or respect. I never liked to give allegiance to anyone, and I still don't want to. I have always been anti-establishment, a rebel, but I didn't know how to rebel against a picture or the person I didn't talk to or see physically every day, or someone who was always watching me, unblinking. He knew everything about me. I sometimes think; that was why we had this burgeoning want to stay out, to play out in the fields, to be refractory to enclosure, because out there we were the Kings and Queens of our world. We didn't have to look up to anyone really. We didn't have to give allegiance to anyone, maybe to a ball made of plastics, which we would chase throughout the day, with only the untamed wilderness watching us, and the gaze of a deer?

But, even in those situations, his dark handsome brooding looks were somewhere down in our subconscious, like our shadows that never left us. And so, we grew up with him watching us, but somewhere in our late school days, somewhere in the late secondary or high school days, we started questioning why he was all over the place, why he was still the president of the country, why we should respect him, why he had to wipe out over 20 000 people from the Matabeleland regions. Yet, for us, there were no alternatives or solutions forthcoming. He stayed in every public place, every radio station, on the television, now with very few jibes and jokes, but still intruding on our privacy. His pictures become embedded in our consciousness. He was our shadow; he refused to leave, even though in our privacy, we had started asking him to leave us alone. The relationship had become fractious.

After school we entered the job market, the reality of it all, was an incredible impossibility, for a lot of us. It was survival of the fittest. Corruption was a scourge and the meltdown had started. People were beginning to be very vocal about their displeasure, and the jokes thickened, jokes made about his pictures. A lot of people were questioning why Mugabe was the centre of all our problems.

"Mugabe must go," was coined by his party's members, but going he refused to go. He told us he wasn't going anywhere, and that, it was his country. Not for the foreigners, not for the whites, not even for us blacks. A lot of people started hanging down his pictures from the walls; some stopped watching television, or even going to national events they knew he would be gracing. Some even had the idea that Mugabe always jinxed national teams, especially the beloved national soccer team, so they started questioning that he shouldn't be attending those games. The rejections mounted on but he refused to leave the televisions, the radios, public places, even on woman's clothing, covering their generous buttocks with his pictures. Some men started asking, or forcing their women to stop wearing those clothes that had Mugabe's face or picture because they didn't want Mugabe to invade and peer at their women's privates. They were jealous of a picture.

I had started developing some sickness with him but I was still tolerant of him. I could still watch him on television, but with gleeful contempt, and would watch his pictures on walls with a slight whinge. I had also started making jokes about him. Even as he aged, he stayed young on the walls. It's his old younger Mugabe pictures that adorned the walls, without showing the changes that had happened to him. and then the tough times came through, late 1990s upto 2009. People, in huge masses, wanted him to go, started to really push him, begging him to go, but he refused to go. He said he didn't want to go. He stayed on the television and the dosage increased until there came a time when we would see or hear about him every five minutes. We simply had nowhere to hide away from him.

I started developing some angry sickness seeing him or his images. I developed hate for him. I still don't like him. Seeing his image made me angry. A lot of people left the country, running away from him; eventually I had to leave, as well. I left for South Africa where I stayed there for two and half years. For the first time he diminished, and he was no longer a constant in my life. For the first time I realised what it meant to be free. I started the healing process. I started to let go of that angry sickness, and the haunted feeling that I got whenever I saw his pictures. I started being normal, the normal that I knew how to be, like liking myself again.

I succeeded and by the time I returned back to Zimbabwe, I didn't have hurtful feelings towards his portraits, but I still didn't like him. I still wanted him to go but I would laugh over it, not to stress over it. He was still there, so many times, on the television, in public places fewer and fewer times, even in my consciousness. Though, the

9

relationship, or lack of, was no longer fractious, or angry, or sickening. He was now like a dead relative I don't like, but who is still talked about by the family. I have to listen to the talk, yet it doesn't hurt anymore having to do that. I think, deep down my conscious, I had to believe he was dead for me to get over him. Only that I knew it hadn't happened, physically. When he dies physically, then I would really start on dealing with the emotionality of it all. I will start really removing him from my consciousness, but at the present moment he is still there.

He is so old, sometimes he shakes, is frail. I believe sometimes he doesn't get up, out of the bed. He is ailing. He is dying, that's why he doesn't bother me. Maybe I will die before him, but it doesn't really matter. He is going. His portraits inside me are dying. He has failed to update my consciousness with a better portrait.

Revisiting: The Portrait Of ...

Mr Scarfman: The body of our revolutionary leader will be buried at the national shrine

ZIFA's washout, the Nephew of the former revolutionary leader shakes his head, let's call him Nephew 1.

Nephew 1: We are yet to sit down as a family and also the chiefs of Zvimba would make the final call!

Nephew 2: Our Sekuru is a chief so he should be buried with other chiefs, not thieves at the national shrine,

Another dreadlocked nephew across Limpopo, after running out of Limpopo river's bones munching crocodiles, blunders in.

Zimbabwean 1: So where are the bones of the old man going to rest?

Zimbabwean 2: I don't give a rat's ass where they are going to bury him. If they were putting his bones on trial á la old Stunned Lake Samkange's *On Trial For My Country*, then I would have been interested. Let them fight over his body.

....

3 years after his funeral the fight over his bones has spiraled in Mr Scarfman's courts.

Court 1: His bones must be exhumed and be buried at the national shrine, at the beautiful national grave we spend millions building for him

His Wife: We are going to appeal the court order!

Court 2: No, his bones should be left lying peacefully in Zvimba, they belong to the Zvimba people.

"What of Tekere's family who were forced to bury their father at the national shrine by these bones when they were still clothed in flesh." Chenjerai Hove, in his *Bones* book doesn't ask from the grave.

And the son of Father Zimbabwe thinks he has seen the light too,

Father Zimbabwe's Son: Since they are refusing with his bones, I would also want to exhume my father's leftovers from the national shrine and bury them in Mthwakazi kingdom!

Dear Robert Mugabe:

Identification with right!
"Enough is enough, what is enough?"

I am on the pyre of my thoughts, burning deep down inside myself, walking on broken boulevards of deterred dreams, trying to find voice to my soul that burns in this fire. And for some time I have avoided using my pen to deal with this burning, now I have no choice. I have decided to use this paper and pen to write you this letter, Robert Mugabe- to live in defiance again. I would like to ask everyone else who reads this letter, every Zimbabwean, everyone who loves Zimbabwe, every friend of a Zimbabwean to join me in this journey. I know this is too small a ripple in a sea of deliberations, but I offer this as one teaspoon at a time, draining, ok I mean disturbing, this ocean.

I know human beings are meaning-oriented beings. We tell stories that explain what is really happening in our lives. We are sick and tired of you, Robert Mugabe. It's not that we didn't love you. It's just that you couldn't love us back the way we did you. It's not that we will never love you again, it's just that we stopped now. Yes, years ago we loved you, looked up to you and supported you. We thought you were brave, wise and beautiful; we believed in the ideas you flipped off like gospel, but there is now nothing to love about you. You have gotten long in the tooth. You have taken our love and shitted on it, on us, day after day, for over 37 years. You still urinate on us and call that trickle-down effect.

All that we have known on our body politic was you as our leader. We were born when you were already our leader, we grew up with you,

13

we became adults, started families, went to college, started careers, only to realize that you had destroyed everything that we fought for, everything that we thought was our country, our future. We have become old men and women with you as our leader, fighting you! Your greedy hands, and the equally greed hands of time moving mercilessly onwards, leaving us with nothing but sorrow, disappointment, anger, remorse, guilty... So what is good left in us to love you with?

We fought you for years and years and you still continued subjecting us under your vicious rule. Haven't we paid enough for allowing you to liberate us? Haven't you taken everything that we thought we also fought for? Haven't you made us villains in our own country, refugees in our homes, and paupers in our land? Haven't you driven us out of the country? You say you fought for us, so did you fight that war to punish us later? Did you fight that war for yourself and your family? We have worked, slaved all our lives and continue to slave under your punitive yoke so that we would earn a living and fund you with our taxes which you use to feed your family; money you steal, money you misuse, money you bastardise, money you use to bleed more money from us like a vicious tokoloshi- becoming an expert in minding your own business! Robert, we have carried you on our backs like lice, whilst you drink our blood dry the way the sun's light bakes dry the earth. Now you have drained our arteries and veins. Robert, we plead with you to leave our political landscape. Just leave us alone. Let us go, please. We will be fine without you. We don't need you. Robert, an active partner looks for the empty lands inside and or between him/her with their partners to fill it up, thus without filling it, they become a worse, more isolating kind of partner!

Robert, you have destroyed and killed everyone who was against you from the moment you came into our world. You pushed out

14

Ndabaningi Sithole from ZANU-PF's helm, and over years you told us Ndabaningi was a sellout and tribalist. Robert, you killed Hebert Chitepo, Josiah Tongogara, Leopold Takawira. I know you say it was the Rhodesians who did that but this is what we have learned to know you do so well. Everyone is wrong, everyone is a tribalist, everyone else shouldn't be the president except you and your family, and everyone is guilty except you, not even until they are proven guilty! Isn't that your ideology? They are guilty until proven innocent! We know you pushed out Nkomo; you killed over 20 000 civilians in Matabeleland, and swallowed Nkomo back, killing him bit by bit for over 12 years. How sad he must have felt all those years working with you, his conqueror, and when eventually the creator took him back from your clutch, how happy he must have been to finally rest far away from your dark painful shadow. You called him a dissident when you fired him. You told us it's him who was wrong; who was plotting to start a war against you and had arms cache hidden at his farm. You told us it's the Ndebele people who were wrong. You killed them in thousands, in broad daylight.

You pushed Edgar Tekere out of ZANU-PF. You were so shameless to push out the one who brought you into the party, the one who gave up his position to accommodate you, and over the years you insulted him and frustrated him until he died a broken man. You told us you were the one who was right, that Tekere was a tribalist. You destroyed Morgan Tsvangirai, insulted him, beat him up, call him names like *Chematama*, jailed him, and attempted to kill him several times. You killed, maimed and pushed millions of Zimbabweans out of the country who supported Tsvangirai, calling them traitors. You killed Tsvangirai's wife, and thus, you killed him. Ever since, he has been a pale shadow of the Tsvangirai we loved and fought for, the last two

15

decades. You killed, maimed and pushed out the white people, taking everything they built for centuries, destroying industry and agriculture. You called them names. You told us they were not Zimbabweans. You extruded them out of the country. Are you Zimbabwean yourself? Is your father's father Zimbabwean? Why didn't you leave too? Everyone knows your father was of Malawi origin, so which Zimbabwe were you talking of? Does being Zimbabwean only equate to blackness! You haunted Joyce Mujuru out of ZANU-PF after you had succeeded in killing her husband, Solomon. You burned Solomon to ashes. You told the whole nation Mujuru was plotting to kill you, to remove you from power, was visiting N'angas, and we still wonder how you got to know that if you were not doing the same thing. You made us be laughing stock. The world laughed at us, that we still visit N'angas, that our leaders still take advice from N'angas on how to run a country. You succeeded in haunting her out.

You have killed, laughed and ridiculed everyone who stood up against you like Simba Makoni, Ndumiso Ndabengwa, Lovemore Madhuku, Tendai Biti, Learnmore Jongwe, Welshman Ncube, Nkosana Moyo, Herbert Murerwa, Ray Kaukonde, Dikamai Mavhaire, Shuvai Mahofa, Didymus Mutasa, Andy Flower and The Zimbabwe Cricket Team, The War Veterans, MDC, Trevor Ncube, Jeff Nyarota and several Newspapers personalities, ZBC, Jestina Mukoko... the list is endless. You called all these counter revolutionary forces, you told us they were tribalistic, were plotting against you. You made yourself a victim every of these moment. You called us to support you against these. Are you the country, Robert? If the whole country seemed to be plotting against you, there is something wrong with what you are doing. Why don't you just leave the country so that people won't plot against you? You have made Zimbabwe your little garden. It's up to you which

16

tomatoes and cabbages need harvesting for food. You have made Zimbabwe to be the poorest country in the whole world. You have made Zimbabwe a laughing stock to the world. Is this the Zimbabwe you fought for? Is this the Zimbabwe you inherited from your fellow Ian Smith? Is this the liberation you made us help you with? Is this the reason why thousands of our brothers, sisters, fathers, and mothers died for? Is this the country your child died for, so that you will make us your prisoners? Don't you feel ashamed with what you have done to us? Do you have a heart, Robert? Are you human, Robert? What makes you wake up every day? How do you confront the wounds you have caused on your fellow countrymen and the country you so loved? Why do you want to continue hurting us? What have we done to you to deserve this anger you have on us? Are you not tired of hearing every child crying your name, every man and woman mourning by your name, every old man and woman mourning under your thumb? How do you lie to yourself every day that the people still love you?

Anger, jealousy, vindictiveness, inferiority and superiority complexes are acts of powerlessness, and are painful, Robert. You feel unworthy of us, Robert. You know you are flawed and cannot be fixed. You want to be loved but feel unlovable. You want to love us but feel that you are incapable of loving. No matter what you do, you still feel it's not enough and that you are incurably inadequate, intrinsically and permanently flawed. You are afraid of us people. You are afraid we now see who you really are. You think without keeping trying to win us over to you, we will not want anything from you. This feeling of powerless in power is the most painful lesson on Earth school, Robert. A bland heart is patternless, Robert. It doesn't smell right once you get a whiff of it. In what hell did you come from? Go back, Robert. Go back to where you came from!

And lately you have pushed out Emerson Mnangagwa. The explanations started flowing in your rallies, explanations that failed to explain, conclusions that failed to conclude. You made yourself into a Moses, the aura of psychic breath, in hot language; you told us Mnangagwa is a traitor, that he is visiting N'angas to kill you off. That he was working against the country, that he wasn't respecting you. Robert, what's there to respect about you? Why do you want to be respected too much? Why are you forcing us to respect you? Why are you changing roads, airport, and calendar days to your name? Respect is earned, Robert!

What respect have you earned from us when we are dying on queues, queuing for our hard-earned cash, dying in streets trying to sell wares, fruits and vegetables for livelihood, dying in our homes of hunger, diseases, poverty; dying in foreign lands far away from home trying to eke out an existence, dying from stress, cardio-vascular diseases and depression, dying from lack of a horizon to migrate to, dying inside ourselves from lack of opportunities to grow, dying trying to remove you from power, dying trying to pay taxes so that your family would have more to loot from us, dying in shame that we destroyed the jewel of Africa with you, that Zimbabwe was! Like me, many things in Zimbabwe have died (tired), from flowing. Are you not satisfied with the blood you have drunk from us. Uri chikwambo here, Robert? (Are you a Tokoloshi, Robert?). Why do you want to keep draining us, until when? We beg you, Robert, go! Leave us alone! We are tired of you, go! GO! GO! There is no ceilings above you anymore, Robert, but open skies full of changes, welcome it, embrace it, leave, GO!

I will continue to write these letters, just to move the air around, until you leave us. I will encourage every Zimbabwean, every friend of a Zimbabwean to join me in this journey. Chara chimwe hachitswanye inda (one finger doesn't kill the lice). I will continue writing these letters as a form of protest. Let's now begin the healing process. It's now or never!

I am the one you killed quietly, now speaking

Thank you, Ndinotenda, Ngiyabonga. I have to thank the spaces…

Rantings Of A Raving Pen

D on't suppose this game is only played in undemocratic societies... It is so wrong to assume so. It is the land versus freedom game that I am talking of! It's always an apology, a favourite story, a heartfelt confession...I would have to start that way. Even in a society where there are "three legs of the iron-pot", if any one of the legs of the iron pot is longer than the other two: It would have powers to make redundant the other two legs, powers to control the other two legs, powers to build a Napoleon behind that shimmering label of democracy... Maybe, that's why my grandmother, and those before her, decided to have clay pots that didn't have legs; to balance things, somehow? To balance things the way a rainbow seem to balance colours on the horizons. Yet sometimes, the beautiful colours of the rainbow myth are a pointer telling us to look beyond their, poet's-sung-about, beauty. Ultimately, their hollowed haunting colours, usually results in one colour playing the god-insect function.

Not even a single one of these players in this game had the right to claim legitimate authorship to the start of that anarchic situation.
No, no, no... It's so stupid and naïve to think that a powerless individual could do that. No! It must have started somewhere..., where a single individual- a single purpose person- is vested with all the powers that begat power; randomly distribute tools of anarchy...
Such as weaponry, total disregard of governing rules, open and conceited manipulation of all the mirrors of a society and naked provocation for violence by a small group controlled by that single

individual. What follows is total anathema. It is this trend..., maybe a pattern; I said a pattern... patterns to aid to my augment! I have to start here. Single purpose individuals: single purpose ideology, is usually the trait of the lunatic..., or is it the fanatic? Then, things will start to take shape? When we try to look at the patterns, when we try to study the patterns, when we try to unlock their frozen meanings..., things begin to take shape. Single purpose individuals plan for every of their moves; every word, every nod, every silence..., everything becomes, (disguised) planned, and patterned events. And, there is another pattern?

He knows that if he sits on his laurels and waits for things to follow their undisturbed course, he will become history. We are talking of single purpose individual. That he will vanish into the gossamer's web of time, and so, he has to refuse to step aside..., and how? There are some things we will never really control; no matter how good we are at controlling things, even when we are non-paralleled at that. We can only harness them. We can only channel them. We have to avoid blocking them..., freedom? Freedom gives some people the right to rule over others and it is only a few of us who are totally alien to this sweet call. The quest of which, can never really be controlled, but maybe; can be harnessed towards a truly altruistic goal. No one can overcome the need to constantly change and re-invent one's self. My apologies to change for calling it a necessity here but barriers against change can gobble up continents, alienate the whole population, swallow ideas and limit future expressionisms. But what else would people need?

He knew they wanted to be free, but he offered them something else..., not in exchange, of course not! He told them it was the only way towards prosperity, towards freedom. It was a delaying or diverting tactic for him. He instilled into the minds of these people the importance of this need, at the sad demise of the other need (freedom). He emotionalised the offer (putting all the spices that he could think of). Indians, my Grandma once told me that they are so good at doing that. Putting spices into food..., umm, it smells great..., putting spices into things too.

What would people need most?

Not freedom, no, not this one on its own, no! Yes, they still want freedom, but it is an untouchable thing. People need a state of happiness and happiness results from a sense of security. In order to be secure, we need to have something that we can see, feel, touch, taste..., at least in our mind... I mean something that one can singularly own to one's self. I would offer them land! He also offered them land, so it must be right to offer them land, somehow. All right, we now have two things..., needs, competing favourably...and unfavourably, too. The Land versus freedom game; it is our game!

How did I come to this pedantic interpretation of events..., and that seer couldn't refrain from assigning it into the narrative convenience dustbin? But of course, accumulated observation of a countless historical examples: Palestine, Egypt, Israel, USA..., suffices enough. How can we offer this land...? Please do it this way and I am so sorry; it is the pedant's sweet call again but don't hate me, at least not too offensively, for this lazy self-indulgence. Sometimes, we just can't help it, being pedantic, I mean. Just tell someone you want to offer him land. Tell someone you want to take his land away. Tell someone that this person owns more land than that one. Tell them that; that land

22

must be taken and be given to them. You are on a dangerously perilous emotional drive. All right, let's drive through and see what would become of that?

Spices..., Indians..., It's a traversing of centuries and centuries..., of good food-spices-eating-fighting-living, of being; and all the hordes are all up in arms, their laughter..., their sweet, sweet anger! Anger: it is the only way the soul could say something or do something…and so he invoked anger. He talked about the wars that were fought for this land. He talked about the sacrifices, the slaughtering, and those mass killing fields... The madness! My apologies: may those who have died be patient with the way my memories have faded, the way I am trying to recall some. Oh, those internecine mass killing fields in the lands beyond still littered with unburied bones and unassigned anger! Here, he was inclosing hollow worlds into words, into being, into lives. I am also sorry for the great question of life for these small answers. But he talked the argument; back, back, further..., and further to the caves... Here, he was disclosing hollow words into whole worlds, by talking about the injustices- that the people suffered from- before they took up arms.
The Serbs do that to their children.

They talk of 1938; they talk of the battle of Kosovo in 1938 against the all-conquering ottoman Turks. Here, I am talking about that hot- red hot spot they call the Balkans. One can come to understand why the Balkans has always been a restless spot that it has been..., land! The Irish talk about the battle of Boyne: and the Palestinians do the same thing to their children. 1948! 1948! 1948!

23

The loss of the Palestinian state and the subsequent birth of the Zionist state! For goodness sake, I am not a Palestinian neither am I an Israeli but the bloody hell; why did they ever got sucked into this game: land versus freedom? Here, we are talking of that powder keg they call the Middle East.

It is a devastating game they have perfected out there; the bones, the bullets, the dust and those biological invasions mixes with anger, rage and revenge. It is within this fund that we draw upon haunting cries of the wounded and the dying. And the morals of these stories are... Nothing should be forgiven. One day make them pay. Now we have an excuse, don't we? We enforce this excuse and everything else can now be side-lined. Nothing now, I mean absolutely nothing..., I said nothing, is more important than this. But he was only emotionalising their needs!

And then there is also another pattern: he is a disguised despot working behind those colours of the rainbow myth which we have talked of; about the haunting colours of the rainbow myth? What would be the best way, of offering that over emotionalised thing, so that it won't appear as if he is belittling their other need? Remember that throughout that process; he wants to appear democratic to a people that are already sadly seeing some glimpses of his undemocratic tendencies. Who really is he? Someone said that if you give name to something, you will unconsciously empower it. With that in mind, let's give him a name and let's call it an act of self-empowerment, indigenisation, maybe that? Maybe an institutional name would do fine..., not that he reveres it, no, not institutions, no.

Executive! Executive! Executive... They seem to be a nice ring to the rhyme of that word. Ok, executive..., and remember the three legs of the iron pot? The executive, the legislature, and the judiciary; he is the executive. He has to involve the other two legs. Suppose the Law-makers can be whipped into line..., after all, there are all controlled by him. They are mostly from the party that he rules..., and implicit here, I am saying that they are from the party he owns. Do you know what one can do with a thing that he owns? Some sage said, (well, I can't remember his name), but he was this man of mountain wisdom..., not Solomon no, of-course not. He said that the best way to harness the unbridled potentiality of a radical element is to offer and deny two or more important things at the same time. That is, Frank Herbert, in, God emperor of the Dune. He wouldn't rule out threats, punishments and killings. After all, he has the power to dissolve their body politic, that is, the legislature. He knows about the survival patterns? The Nazi holocaust had collaborators. Idi Amin and Bokassa re-invented the Nazi's boxing up things (putting (things, people) into boxes) mentality in Africa. In the same vein they created collaborators too.

He can control the judiciary by boxing them up, and whilst he still has an upper hand, he let others of the like-minded ideology to his own, craft some piece of paper, bill, legislature... Name it whatever you might want to, but he runs it through the now gagged Law-makers. The proper judiciary (not the one that has crafted this bill) can as well bloody sing whilst waiting for their chance. After all he has also involved some of them, them judges into creating this charade of a constitution. How could some learned judges, who really understood the idea of the three legged pot, still keep most of the powers (executive powers) in the same person, who had been abusing the powers, that the whole country has been hue and cry over? If it is not political cowardice, I don't know what it is?

He now has the law that he wants; he is rolling. Who else can stop him now..., who really can stop him? He encompasses the tin pot bill (the land bill) into the whole hog-wash. In so doing, he changes the whole law into something that would make him an untouchable. By the other things he has done, by uncontrollable things like freedom, by his failures and follies. It's easy to do that: he searched around for people who could do that for him. People who still believed in him, people who were his followers, people who were afraid of him, people who wanted to selfishly enrich themselves, people who were painfully dying to do him a service, people who were... It's a people, people, people landscape that he created, but it was also a power base that he re-created in the process.

Expect insanity. Expect dangerous thoughts and extremities.
Expect anything that can be done under the sun. Expect stupidity at its unprecedented showing. Sing like a parrot; inaccessible songs are dreams that never get away. Dance like a parrot; it feels like the music can be heard around the world, so dance to its rhythm. Talk like a parrot. Here: he recreates a lower grade-class going through its P.E class. Moi (that Daniel Arap Moi fellow who once ruled that little black water country called Kenya) was in this lower class-grade for some time, and he sang unabashedly, with a beautiful boy's tenor voice, the songs he was taught to sing by the enormous bass voice of the Uhuru (Kenyatta?) himself. He sang songs that were readable in the language of a fading or lost generation. And his music, in self-conscious superposition, was breathing through his mouth. Never was there ever

26

such a beautiful boy, and for some long unforgotten winters he tantalized us with his genius, but one day he woke up with a sore mind and a dead voice. Sadly for us fellows who had fallen in love with his songs.

Whilst we are still at that, and word of advice fellows: don't ever include, in this parroting choir of yours, players (praise singers) who would do you de-service. Find a way to exclude them..., by the way, don't just extrude them, but if anything, extinguish them! Since he had all the powers that begat power, this wasn't such a terribly blowing headache for him. But he also wanted to appear democratic? He went back to the people! For other disguises, he asked for the people's opinions on this tin-pot constitution that he had now drafted.

This was another opportunity for him, he is the executive, remember that; to white-wash the people by overly repeating..., incessantly... I said incessantly, how important it was for this very important thing to be valued importantly by everyone. He had the spin doctors (a mad professor) to do that for him; telling the whole nation that they had to embrace this tin pot constitution. This mad professor would cut everyone who was against this tin pot thing to pieces, for voicing their disagreeable taste

The people had to eat breakfast on it, elevenses on it, lunch on it... Supper, breath, drink and sleep on it... They even had to dream on it, dance to it..., singing those convoluted revolutionary songs on it. Dancing and singing like they were dancing to those songs of autumn nights, nights of carousal. Remember, he had manoeuvred everything else in the constitution to suite his needs by enshrining well this very

27

important element (need), the land. He architected a bogus constitution (the one that kept all the executive powers to himself)..., one that could protect him in the future. He consulted with the people and in so doing; he was enhancing his public relations with the people. Are we to think that he made a mistake by doing all that? Anyone can be excused for being polemical here, for in human terms, evidence alone without judgments is pretty inadequate.

Ok; let's try to map the landscape of his thinking. Don't we think it was all a manoeuvre? It showed him some home truths? People showed him how capable they were at determining what was right from what was wrong. They showed him that they were not the gullible sorts he thought they were. They knew what they had been doing all along, have always known, would always know, wouldn't be blackmailed anymore... could see through this deceitful plan. They rejected it! I said, they rejected it..., so resolutely. Here, much would depend on how one interprets these results. People, people..., people... On a scale of Zero to One where Zero rates the unthinking, I would have to give them One or any number closer to One on this one. That means I have to give the mad professor a number closer to Zero or Zero itself, just for thinking he could hoodwink an entire nation into supporting this tin pot constitution.

But, as I have already told you that suppression of the incompatible is his greatest trait, that he has the Orwellian big brother mentality, the Nazi's storm trooper mentality, the terrifying invader mentality, the Idi Amin occultist's edge. His other hand; that which is out of sights of the people, is sinisterly moving things beyond everyone's entranced eyes... Moving the land of risk into being again! Whilst he is doing this, the people have now forgotten that single purposes individuals don't like to have their plans disturbed, or else they would go into permanent disarray. With this one, it's a different tune altogether. Tunes! Songs! The Parrots!

He is not into Bach, Brahms..., and neither Beethoven's ninth symphony. Even though he would tell the people that he likes Beethoven's ninth symphony; their viola and violin creates musical colours that are both bright and expressive, but also melancholic and volatile... Their music dripping from those twiggy fingers like late February rains..., no he doesn't like their music? They make a philosophical sound that allows some distances to ponder about the earth and the sky at long ranges. They also have the ability to reach and evoke the arena of timelessness. It is for these qualities that they were not his cup of coffee. He would rather they were momentous tunes, like pop music, like dancing to pop music, popping unto its curled up dimensions, too. So that he would make his own tunes and let others dance to them... thus pop-ishly keeping things in today's language. Oh, wise man makes proverbs and fools repeat them!
Whilst we are still at this proverbial parallelism, apply this nonsense to songs too. We have just discovered him mortals! Best wishes!

Before his songs were confused, disturbed, I mean his plans... he was already breaking new ground and looking at those disturbed songs from dry ground emotionally...and unemotionally. His feelings, emotions and moods are nothing seen before. They tower beyond dreams, myths, imaginations and explanations. They are smooth when he is under terrible obstructions, like the river when it empties into the sea. They soar dangerously, rage formidably, and soar violently when he

29

is not under obstructions. He likes obstructions and he doesn't like them, in one and the same breath. He can be complete opposites in room enough to change invariably from one form to another, or even being contrasts at the same time.

Ahhh..., can't we speak silently, and be silent at the same time?
Happy and sad! Beautiful and ugly..., at the same moment, and why not...What is beauty? Is this that we disagree about or it is about what ugly is? Greening around the core, no..., not greening no, but maybe greying or decaying in the core and exuding strengths all around the outer edges. These are just a pail of words which although pretty archaic aren't bad at all, are they? Aren't they a terrible beauty, too; is it ugly? Maybe both... and I said at the same moment. There are lives within him which he couldn't keep under check. He exudes dimensions, edges, bottoms and depths.... He is a brute force of nature unleashed with medieval anger on any human dissent.

Ok, ok, ok; I stop it!

I would have to go back to the beginnings of this writing, to find the wellsprings of these ravings, again. Would you; you, who are reading these Rantings of the raving pen, let me go back a little bit with my ravings? Please! I know I am asking too much from you, but please would you lend me about two or three years. Ok, I know I am being too self-indulgent, but if you would allow for that, just this moment, then I would start on it.

He would allow groups to form. After all, isn't that so beautiful watching them growing. He would allow groups to form whatever are their intentions. He would let them evolve and wield some stupid powers over him. Obviously they would be demanding for something as a smock screen to their actual (veiled) intentions. He couldn't give them anything straight away! A little bit of sweat is good here and, he lets it all come closer to their extremities, but not beyond. Such that they would almost dream that getting what they want is heaven-status or anything as closer to that, as is possible. Just like some traveller in an endlessly ice-capped land could dream of, and at the same shiver; equate heaven-status to any kind of warmth.

When people fail to realize their ambitions they inflict pain on themselves and ultimately, on that that has been denying them such fulfilment. He allows them to demonstrate some of their anger and vapid power before they get to a dangerously volatile condition. He has, all along, been denying them things ...and all of a sudden, at the flicker of a second, he is accepting all their grievances..., so apologetically, so regrettably, so genuinely... he also offers more of whatever they have been demanding for.
He just gives them money.

It's a sucking mentality that he creates with this group. No, he doesn't really create it. The mercenaries have been there before him, so he is just harnessing this historical invention. He leaves them in dangerous disarray, in confusion too, because at the moment, they are now bloating themselves on the Captain's right to booty, which he has just awarded them. There are now a small group controlled by this powerful single purpose individual. In the same vein, at the same time, they have forgotten all their other interests, but the loot, of-course, only the loot! Sadly they now permanently equate everything to a monetary value.

With unequalled speed, whilst everyone is celebrating..., the people who have caged his ambitious tin pot constitution and this small group he now controls. I said with speed..., immeasurable! He throws the spanners at work. All of them are his...the spanners, the people, this group, and I said all of them. So, this group owes him a favour? I remember something and some philosophy... There is this old Chinese philosophy that says if you save someone from death, that someone you have saved would now belong to you. It would be your obligation to look after them, their lives, their loves and their happiness, too. You can ask for anything and they would simply have to give it to you; whatever it is that you have asked for. So that they might as well happily shout on top of the mountains saying that they were not occupiers of the farms but land redistributors and nation builders for him. They would do that for him. Do we see the things that we can do with (to) the things that we own! I said, he threw all the spanners at work.

He throws this group onto the people. All the seven hells and all the fires! I said all the seven hells and all the fires. Oh, I can hear someone whispering about eight hells... and yes, even that and don't forget the fires, the fires, the fires! It burns, let it burn, let it burn, let it burn! Rome might as well burn, for all that he cares!

He targets an element of this people and unearths that emotional (never to forgive) concept once again, striking all the way back to those tiny-tiny cellular beginnings. After all, they don't belong here! It's either

32

there are black for them to belong here or they would just as well go to hell. But, why is it that we do not want to forget? The Fools! The past! Forgiveness..., forgetting. It's a full spectrum of the impossible tribalistic tendencies that are brought forth for us to share in. So foul, and so full of the ages! Maybe there is always security with the ages..., and the past too. We know everything because someone once experienced it and expressed it. Someone also kept it in their tribal memories, thus in ours too. It's quite different with the future because there is no knowing what the unknown would turn out to be. Maybe that's why people prefer living in the past; or it's because they fear what they don't even fear, which is not fear itself, but maybe the reason for fear..., which is, "just being there."

But he should have known that it is a fool's myth to believe in the use of the sword as the basic instrument of governance. He should have known that a sword can only lock a person into a predictable pattern of behaviour, that the sword would incite heroism from the oppressed.

Hitler tried it on the Jews and Europe and it exploded. The Soviets tried it and it rotted in Moscow's gutters. London tried it on the colonies, and it burned to ashes in Africa. History is replete with many other examples, but whilst we are still interpreting these results let's muse... by maybe estimating the possibilities of this historical agency.

Just a little bit.

And this was his only apology

"It was a moment of madness"
Which one, is our question?

Dear Morgan Tsvangirai:

Don't be used again!
"A ball that is a ball will always be a ball."

Inanimate objects move only in dreams and fables, but in this letter I am going to move an inanimate object, that is, a ball. The soccer ball is round and made so that it would roll on the ground in a fair way, and will travel a bit slower in air than other balls like the rugby and American football balls. Balls! The soccer ball's life is unenviable. As I noted it travels more than the other football balls...yes Rugby is football, American football is football, so are the two funny obscure footballs: lacrosse and Australian Rules football. Okay, let stick to soccer. A soccer ball is overused as it only stays in the hands of the players for a few minutes, mostly protected by the goalkeeper; if the goalkeeper is not bouncing it off the ground, trying to figure who to kick the ball to. It is kicked for 90 plus extra minutes, it is thrown tens of times, handled several times, it travels the pitch more than all the 22 players plus substitutes combined together; it is hit, it hits players, goal posts, the ground, gets bumped. And at the end of the game, it is thrown away, left alone until the next game.

It becomes an object at rest, it stays at rest until acted upon by these players again. The 22 plus players, their coaches, the supporters, get more out of the work of the ball; limelight, awards, respect, community etc... As the games pile up the ball, it builds the players' profile, the coaches, administrators etc... The supporters are happy. Are you happy? Morgan, I feel you are the ball that the country's players have used each time they play their games! I am sorry for insulting you but I have to write this burning letter to you. It is a narrative that oscillates between the gentleness of the falling showers of rain and the wearing off of hope after disaster, bringing haunting truth and beauty pulled through memory. It is a timbre of memory of sound, and these memories are layered: a sound, smell, a sight: a kind of remembering, a witnessing, a gathering!

Look at the beautiful years and the work you did over the years at Zimbabwe Congress of Trade Unions. How you transformed a small government organisation into a formidable foe to Robert Mugabe's government. How you went toe to toe with Robert Mugabe who had goons behind his back to protect him against you. For years you fought, you were the ball the workers, the politicos and industry played. Yes, it helped you to form the MDC, and this accorded you a lot of respect by the Zimbabweans- so did some other balls in life, like a baseball ball that was Jack Robinson, and the basketball that was Michael Jordan etc.... The world over became aware of you, but the games never stopped on you.

You entered another game: the people of Zimbabwe versus Robert Mugabe and his party who were now the two opposing teams. They played you for years on end until you finally had a chance to retire, to wallow in glory like Michael Jordan's balls. No, not those you are thinking of! You won *fair and square* the March 2008 elections, false ushering in a brand new year at a time when we believed that sort of thing, in scheduled change. Some still say you won enough to form a government, but one of the goons, one of those players refused you rest. Mugabe's goons pushed you back into the game and changed the

36

game on you and the other players. They started playing Australian rules football, by using the American football ball whilst the people were still using the soccer ball. I told you the soccer ball travels slowly in air than the American football ball. And the American football ball is built in way that it bounces off or rolls off unfairly on the ground. Also the American football ball can be thrown and kicked willy-nilly, as long as it is going forward. Also Robert didn't care about you, the soccer ball, but the people. American football players rough it more than the soccer players, and Robert's goons played rough brutal games on the people who were still playing their soccer ball. You are the people. Robert cheated you by killing players of the opposition. And then grabbed you into his strangling hands and told the world they had to recognize him as the winner since he had taken you hostage. He told the world he would give the people a few of his substitute players. He gave the people a few ministries to butter the world with a reason why he had to keep you in hostage. The world accepted him as the winner of a no contest game and awarded him the trophy. At the end everyone had to accept these conditions. Morgan, you were so gullible to allow Robert to put you in his personal collections/trophies counters, in his Munhumutapa offices. To the outside world, to the opposition- to the people; he told them he is taking good care of you as you rested.

But that was all a lie's white truths- so black, Morgan! He played games with you in his Munhumutapa offices, games he had played and won against Nkomo, whilst he legitimized his presidency. He allowed his first team players he had kept in the GNU government to play more games on you. And those players he hadn't kept in the government were set on the people, to turn the people into supporting Robert. You were played left and right until Robert Mugabe felt he could revert back to the soccer game with the people. Until you had cleared the bills and the financial issues that had accumulated whilst Robert slept like a disease and an ill-fitting cure. I mean until you had righted the economy for him in the GNU years, until you had helped him mend his party that was in tartars after the March 2009 elections, until he had won more people to his side.

The people and Robert decided to create a new constitution for their future games on you. But what you never realized more and more of the people distrusted and lost faith in your abilities as a leader. They begin to question the linesman; referee etc, saying the ball they were using had been overused and tempered with by Robert during the GNU years. What Robert did was to kill everything that made you strong, and removed air from you; you became floppy and flappy. He allowed you to make stupid flops like those woman escapades, the corruption of your councilors..., and made capital out of the flops. All these you did because Mugabe had tempered with you. You became an operatic version of a crow, a blue jay figure skating in a blue custom flying only when the wind blows, and the wind was Mugabe. So when the people decided to reverse fixtures in 2013, Mugabe trusted you more than the people. The people decided to field a weak team, didn't even prepare for the match, and were busy scrutinizing you and what Robert had done to you. Robert used this combination of a flattened ball that you were and the bored weak opposition to win the 2013 match, and discarded you as he formed his government with a full team and reserves, taking back all those positions he had given the people during the GNU years. You simply didn't amount to diddly!

He continued with his games on his team. This time he decided to push his team, each against the other. He created a new game. He created new camps, and the leaders of these camps were Emerson Mnangagwa and Joyce Mujuru. Since he was tired and ageing he decided to rest a bit and created a part-player, part-referee, part-boss on the game, in his wife. She played the games on his behalf, against Mujuru and Mnangagwa. Robert rested. Morgan, you also rested and nursed your wounds. This new game was vicious and was played with one gun (Robert) in the hands of this player, Grace Mugabe. The other players had no weapons. She played the game of elimination. Grace used the AK47 to kill off half the players and Mujuru in 2014 and replaced these with her favored younger players, some say for sex (playoffs) payoffs, and these were set on Mnangagwa. Mnangagwa was knocked out. What it did was to make everyone realize Mugabe was a ruthless bastard. Grace killed everyone, killed the government, killed the party, and killed the country. Yet Grace and Robert underestimated the power of Mnangagwa as he went scuttling, hiding- it was said he went to a land of strength to the east and then south, and in the southern lands he returned back wielding battalions and battalions of goons that descended on Robert. Morgan, I know whilst all these things were happening you were now fighting a different game in your party and person. This game is dangerous too as it involves biological invasions deeply inside your body and party. You are fighting an illness, how it is wearing your body down, gnawing second by second at your will, a pounding suffocating pain surfing away a mountainside, eating you down until escape into the pitch becomes the only lover you want to hold now.

I have heard you are back at work, Morgan; hanky-panky all over, strutting like a cock. You have been asked to come back to the pitch again. Those players, Robert's team and the people, have missed kicking you around. They are telling you that you are the best ball they ever had. I am surprised you have forgotten you were recuperating, you were not even fit enough to lead your own party, have barely tried to connect with the electorate, to win back all those people Robert pushed away from you during the GNU. You have adopted more new balls in your party to strengthen your chances of not getting kicked as you are ill, but they have picked on you again. Are you fit to be played for another 5 years by these players who now seem to have multiplied since Robert opened the can of worms…, I mean his armpits. Morgan, know that they are going to play you rough for the next 5 years. Know that this time they will kill you, one way or another; know that by the end of the 5 years no one will bother about you ever and your new balls. Yes, they want you to legitimize the whole charade and their thuggery, of a game they have been playing. Yes, you will right the economy for them again, the country, the party etc.., and then they will discard you off for the last time. Nobody will touch you again. This is what they did to Ndabaningi Sithole, Edgar Tekere, to Joshua Nkomo, to everyone the people had loved. A big question on my mind is, are you genuinely in opposition to Mugabe or it's just been a game you played on us. Are you a boy who caught a falling star in his hands, who liked the way it purpled his palms, deepened the shallow tracks of his lifeline. Why do you keep trying to save Robert and ZANUPF from disappearing into oblivion?

Morgan, you should have said no and refused to enter the GNU in 2009, that was used by the army and Robert to stay these thugs and thieves in power. Understand it is the army that has been playing Robert and you all the past 10 years. It was the army that told Robert not to resign when you beat him fair and square in 2009, and cooked a situation, whereby a GNU was a process they used to right the party they so died for. What did the army tell you when you won? They told you Zimbabwe can only be won by the gun, not the pen. What did they tell Robert just some few days ago? The country is for the gun. Only those who fought in the liberation war have the right to lead the party and government. What makes you think the army will change their tone when you win. Now see how they have deposed off Robert, their own leader, because he refused to follow their instruction. You are nobody to the army, Morgan. You are just some sponge that's going to be used to stay the goons in ZANUPF. You were stupid to enter the GNU when at that moment you had Robert and the army by their balls. It's a different kind of balls I am talking of here! In the process you defrauded people of their right to see Robert off forever.

You think it's a different game. It's easy for you and your other balls to be fooled by the situation and think Robert, Mnangagwa and the army are done. No, they want to buy time to sort their messy home. They have realized this game of bullets they were playing in their party has destroyed the party. What you are going to do is to allow them to defraud the other team, the people of their right to vote these thugs out of the government, in a few months' time.

Like I said before, 10 years ago, in other writings before this one, you must refuse to enter this charade of a game. Let them finish each other off. Let them destroy the party completely. Stay safe and wait for the elections which the constitution guarantees. Tell your other balls to pump air up, and go back to the people and win them over. Focus on your party, believe it is broken, and fix it! Prepare your party for the elections next year. Demand for elections to be held next year as per the constitution of the land. Refuse to enter the GNU. I am afraid you would contract a wretched disease that Nkomo contracted- inflamed patriotism of the cerebral membranes, syphilis of spirit, a patriarch of dead organs. They will absorb you into the ZANUPF party and our blessed dream we fought for, for multiparty democracy, will revert back to a one party state of ZANUPF/MDC, just like what happened when

ZANU swallowed Nkomo's ZAPU to form the monster that is ZANUPF and the Zanunisation of Zimbabwe. Insist on the constitution. These thugs have messed what you built during the GNU, now they want you to help them stay. Morgan, you know what's in the basement of ZANUPF - only an idiot would go down there, and you know equally well, though you believe you are not in fact an idiot that you are going to go down those stairs again to the basement. Tell the people to stay stronger. It's only a matter of 8 months, and then they can help you clean out ZANUPF, Robert, Mnangagwa and the goons, off our streets. The truth is they are not going to allow you to win after you have helped them stay in power for another 5 years. Do the skies ever open out to transparency. For goodness sake, you never went to war.

Siya vaurayane nokusunguna (leave them as they kill and jail each other). Leave them to implode. Don't forget its these who destroyed the country and MDC, and when they had succeeded in destroying the country, why didn't they ask you join them in government after the last elections; like they are doing to you now. After all it's the ZANUPF that is dead. Zimbabwe must be fixed through elections, not through building back ZANUPF. Leave Constantine Chiwenga and Mnangagwa to create their own government and it would be null and void in a few months' time. Beyond that they won't be recognized by the constitution and SADC. Leave Mnangagwa to create his power hungry cabinet, and leave Chiwenga to continue with a coup that is not a coup. I didn't say don't support any moves that do away with the monster Mugabe, no. Support them but don't be fooled into joining them in the proposed GNU. The letter might seem to be saying you shouldn't help them destroy themselves, but know that always in accounts of anything, much is left unsaid in order to make what is retained more capable of being focused. Don't enter the GNU! I have cried out louder so that silence won't betray all that we have worked so hard to avoid: death of multiparty democracy in Zimbabwe.

They have only a few months of constitutionality, and beyond that fight them, get help from the international community, force them to do elections. You will now win; their games have restored faith in your supporters to vote them out. Those goons are done and dusted. Now recuperate and if you are fine, go to your party and lead them to the elections. Engage the people. Tell them you have their backs now. Show us how much you have changed. Because if ever we agree to return to your world again, it would be on the condition that you did pass through panel beating, and you are now wiser and changed. Please, stop this tomfoolery. Don't be used again. Don't lose this country again. You are our hero. You are endowed with great destiny, which corresponds with the level of your epicness and with the aid of the gods, your success is inevitable. And a character all the more heroic as you are is more inclined towards mastering the forces which lie outside the scopes of your naked human personality like the strident Jeremiahs of the Old Testament. Rule the day, Morgan. Leave the night to Mugabe and his goons, the ZANUPF. All the pain we were subjected to for the last 4 years will be for nothing as we help you build back the goons. You are the bridge that connects us, that should wait to connect us to consciousness again. The elections are around the corner!

I know you and your balls are power hungry like Robert and his thugs but know that posterity will simply laugh you off as a fool who stumbled on a good thing and messed it. I know all these prohibitions in this letter will only be mere echoes in a void, they will fill nothing. Your heart is set on joining the charade again. Your gullible hands don't feel my epoxy melting; will sign off to another GNU, unfurling the illusion again. But I really feel sorry for you, and that's why I had to write you this letter. Posterity will blame you for allowing power hungry monsters to steal their future. You will become a giant that was destroyed by hubris, like Othello, Macbeth, Kane etc…. your response is predetermined. It is trained like B.F Skinner's rats. The argument in this letter has everything to do with morality, you have a choice. Try to make people you know happy this time, and the conscience of a nation is the gift of its individuals. You have no mandate to be party to this. Stay out of it and save yourself and your party.

I am the ball they played more than you, now I refuse to be played again

NB. I want to encourage fellow Zimbabweans to fight this new game in town, to refuse to become party to it, to continue persevering and fighting for the next 3 months to elections, to organize themselves for the vote, to not embrace another shortcut that will be a long way to freedom again. 3-8 months are not as harsh as 5 stable years followed by another 4 harsh years to another election. Reject this nonsense! Say NO to the monster that the GNU is! The hard work of moving forward must be done as our grief becomes the new homes where we will live until freedom's breath of winning the elections inspires every house, every song, in every street in Zimbabwe.

Thank you, Ndinotenda, Ngiyabonga, to the hand that held this pen!

Laughings Of The Mad Dog

The critic's fodder is such that you will hear them, one after another saying that the writer should "show", not "tell", a story. I suppose it should then be known as story-showing, not storytelling... How can one show his own death? I feel one should only have a ruminative mind, a mind seething with images, a mind made up of small kindling and a living conscience. Their story would play at the boundary of their self-reflexive despairs. They would tell their stories: stories that are fantastic pointing fingers.... straight, strong, complex; a compass arrow pointing south. One has to tell a story as if it's something that hasn't been told before, as if it's unknown, unacknowledged, unrecognised.

The telling should be doors that open and converses. The doors are the cul de sac meanings in the story. One has to tell a story from roads inaccessible, words unbidden, lines untold, and juxtapositions untried...

Ok, I stop it! It could happen in those far-off strange lands but surely not in our beautiful green island. They should simply keep their cold wastelands to their own minds or to themselves. We will keep our own warm beautiful island garden. No, no, no. Never ever here, no, it will never happen here. "Not in our lifetimes, no."

"Ha ha ha he he..."

There is a difficulty with those of the two-legged kind on how to start telling a story, especially if it's a true life's story... A collage of phrases strung together with bits and pieces of meaning, of their own life's story, is not good enough.

"Not with our kind no, no..., no..., no..."

"Ha ha ha he he he..."

Everything, no matter what it is, we start by laughing it off. "Ha ha, ha." And if you can show a story then telling a story is the laughter's country. Laughing things off throws one into the fray. The risk is that it might touch the eye of the censor. Telling a story becomes a problem here. Simply saying these things introduces consequences where there was none. I know that you think we are incapable of this..., of telling a story, that we don't have the source of this jellied laughter in our beings, are we really incapable? You can't even imagine a cat playing poker at that. It doesn't seem to go with you; does that seem to go with you? "Ha ha ha he he..."

As if you should know how we laugh, how dogs laugh, especially how I laugh myself. We even laugh at your funerals; after all, it's none of our business.

"Ha ha ha he he ja urri-uii- ii..., so funny ha ha." But how do humans laugh? One's laughter, like misery for the humans, is seeing hopelessness and futility in their own laughter. Humans!!

46

So funny...ahh, so funny the world that I see in my glittering eyes.
But can an eye see itself? How come I know that mine are glittering yet
the muse have sung about how they never saw the whites of their own
eyes..., and how about those that glitters? My mind seems to take over
and give facts the colour yellow, the yellow glitter in facts, in eyes, too.
That old fool could only cuss, "all that glitters is not gold."

"Ha ha ha..., some glittering nonsense, those ones are so funny."

So funny the world that's been there since I started laughing, it's so
funny. I have started laughing and laughing since those two-legged
creatures started making these sad..., abysmally sad episodes. "Have
you ever seen anything so sad?"

"So...oh, so funny, ha ha ha he he ja?"

I used to think that they are so stupid, so incapable of the deeds they
were now revelling in, with an insatiable hunger. A hunger to do again
and again, a hunger...,

"Ha ha ha he he ja..., such hunger!" As if they have gone crash, crash,
crash..., and landing, imploding! They stand on their two legs and see
what they are doing right now! Just look at it! Just look at that!

"Ha ha ha"

"Tshki tshki tshki..., aha so sad."

47

There is this one. He must be the head of this family..., and do I have to say my family? "No! No, no, no, never!"

Is there any need for us to swear, is there?
Never! Never ever! Never! I have never felt I belonged to this family. About him...; he is way past the age that runs and runs yet he seems to be young..., in fact an infant at that. I am not the one who is saying this. Please don't assign it to me, because he said that himself; that he is a young-old man, or old-young man. I suppose it's between these two..., old-young or young-old, man or maybe the two in one and the same place..., person..., maybe...

"Ha ha ha!"

It's just as well it is word play or it could have driven the be-Jesus down my spine. Just think of that... Young and old, Old and young. Young and old, old and young..., the rhyme of those contrasts..., polarities..., the madness too. Ahaa-a! Ok, to bugger with the shivers..., those be-Jesus, too. Let's muse about the other side of this coin.

Well! Well! Well! It's that Well..., with water creaking out from every pore to no particular direction at all..., those waters! Those waters..., in which we sense something..., otherworldly..., something, something..., something nether worldly.

"Ahaa..., ha ha ha." To describe such a simple thing we could go to such lengths, but hell, come to think of it. "Ha ha ha." Let's think about it ahaa..., just awhile like an offish thought, after all we shouldn't deny the intellect such offish pleasures.

It could really get to be true; that he was incapable of calling his mother's name, always smiling and smiling, crying and crying, cooing and cooing like an infant that he was..., like the dove..., that he was, was he not? It's even truer when one looks at the things that he does whenever he tries to show how little he has aged... As if by this show he would unconsciously be prolonging ageing or maybe his reckoning of the fact that he was old. Show in itself is protection! Protection, yes..., but from what? Why would we need protection? "Ha ha ha."

Protecting one's self from confronting the inevitable reality. "But is there a need for us to build high walls around ourselves." Reality sometimes stinks..., pinpricks..., this bloody reality, the bloody hell it is.

See what the Berliners did to themselves, and they learned it the harder way, I should think so. The Israelites are at it, again, like the Germans, building their own walls, not only physical walls. Ok, let's dibble a bit with the facts: It would cost them over 2 billion dollars at Qalandia which is the gateway between Ramallah and the East Jerusalem. The wall's width is between 30 and 150 metres. These are just facts, but the deeper meaning is trying to know how it feels like, I mean the wall, how it smells, what it does to the one who is encased inside it and the one who is looking at it from the outside, what it does to your head. You may really need to walk through it to really understand it, but if you are Palestinian you need a permit to get through it to be in Jerusalem. There is also the emotional wall to talk of that both Israel and Palestine has to deal with. That physical wall also takes shape even in the streets of Westbank and Hebron, where some streets are exclusively reserved for Israelites. It also reminds me of the old

Salisbury during UDI period, which was an adopted form of apartheid South Africa where in the First Street, blacks were not allowed to walk in. Apartheid South Africa had its own versions and to a lesser extent, it still has the walls in the streets of a free South Africa.

"I won't talk of 'in the minds of a free South Africa', Ha ha ha, humans can always hide things that well, don't they?"

Walls have always been enacted to protect humans from alien invasions; in fact they built walls to surround their fragile beings against the harsh affront of the reality. There is always too much self-indulgence in pity when they lock themselves inside those walls.

"Ha ha ha..., so many words leaping from this tiny shell..., such reasoning!"

Ok, I now agree, let's ask the minds that be. And my anti-civil self silently protests; Don't trust the experts, they know too little of everything else and too much of a particular thing.

"Ha ha ha he he ja." And let's give first preference to the Prophets of psychoanalysis. Freud! Freud! Freud! There was that time when man thought he was God, god, a demiurge…, and created his own godhood clustering… Jung, Laing, Marcuse…. I will resituate Freud's Dora into this. I don't know whether I have to buy into the repressed sexual fears that deprived that upper class Viennese girl of the use of her limbs (what limbs Freud?).

"Ha ha ha ha!" Limbs, hey?! It all started with Freud and here is the landscape of his own thinking or psychosis. He believed that childhood sexual inhibitions influenced future human behaviour. Just that small statement, Freud, and I won't allow you to repress me here; surely you can't let me hang forever in your phallic stage. I would have to ask your grave, if anything, whether children, do feel, at all, sexual?

"Ha ha ha..." I have since told you that these fellas are quite dangerous. They should simply suffer the same fate that dogs have always suffered from..., death, dying..., by hanging, maybe that. Ok Freud, I want to believe you, say had you talked about food..., maybe, maybe that this dog didn't have enough food in its teens. That this dog had gone through harsh treatments when it was still a cub. That this dog...; that, its mother had died when it was still young and that it had taken it the harder way and enclosed itself off. This stuff is believable Freud.

Believe me fellow, it is!

So we now have some reasons for building high walls around ourselves and wallow unchecked in this terrible inner field of self-disgust and recrimination? His fellows were even a lot more ingenious at building the walls that Freud had first enacted. Jung discovered, "the unconscious as an essential source of creativity and mental archetypes as the source of myth, dream and art..." And, I couldn't refrain from laughing at the Jungian inspired psychological dimensions...and the madness too. The; Sensing-Intuiting, Thinking-Feeling, Extroversion-Introversion, Judging- Perceiving paired dimensions, and madness, too. It's a big stroll in the psychological park with a lazy afternoon sun red in the sky. "Baa baa black sheep, have you any wool. Yes sir, yes sir..."

You know that old old clang and old Marcuse intoned about, "sexual desires and instincts as impulses which influenced human society..."

"Ha ha ha." And just listen to the gospel of isolationism from Liang. "We are bemused and crazed creatures, strangers to our true selves, to one another, and to the spiritual and material world-mad even from an ideal standpoint, we can glimpse but not adapt. We are born into a world where alienation awaits us..." Oh no, no, no, drivel! Drizzle, drizzle..., those showers..., those effervescent March showers and the beautiful sun shining on my back. Day dazzle, night noon, shower-shine, and to listen to this cold-cold blustery front, aha...a, drizzle, drizzle, those showers shinning against the setting sun..., and raining upon this rolling world.

And, Liang continued, "...we are potentially men, but are in an alienated state, and this state is not simply a natural system..."

"Ho, Liang, ho...ha ha ha." And, he couldn't stop. "...alienation as our present destiny is achieved only by outrageous violence perpetrated by human beings on human beings." Phew! And, he called that, "The politics of experience". I will not try to cross swords with you Liang for I am too small and you are, were, a Giant of your time. Only one question suffices, fella ...or two.

"Who, then, isn't alienated, fella; and why are you complaining? How about us dogs?"

Ok, fella, and I couldn't help the third aiming..., and questioning,

"How about this mad dog?"

Someone is saying these are the laughings of a very mad dog? Maybe there are, but isn't madness an extreme form of alienation and the mad of your world could even think that madness in method results in absolute genius because it is always a reservoir of surprises.
But, by the way, who would say he is normal..., and then, I suppose, he isn't, in any way, at all..., human; but maybe a mad dog like this one.

And another take! Philosophers! Descartes! Russell! ..., and their own godhood clustering...

"Oh, no, no, before I get my teeth into this fleshy sensorial rich meat... but my top tooth is already sinking into the flesh of my lower lip...and on a lighter note, did you know that for all his genius, and in his lifetime, Freud couldn't afford a pair of suit for himself."

"Ha ha ha hee..."

So, I welcome you all into the Cartesian fantasy. How did he know he existed? How do you know that you exist, yourself? Yes I am asking you!

"Why these questions, in the first place, fella..., what was the motivation..., what are you trying to achieve? Ok, I stop the questionings, but..." Let's hear him out though.

53

"I, myself, did exist since I persuaded myself of something." So, you see to this fella, it was only a matter of persuasion. Don't suppose I am laughing because this is not a laughing matter, in effect, I am mind boggled. I should not have asked you how you, yourself, came to know that you were alive..., or that you existed to the boot.

The question, the answer to, defeats me. But, would you please stop whinnying about that stupid standard contrivance of you being the mirror of yourself. It's too shallow and naive; after all, what mirror will you be using?

So, Descartes persuaded himself and moved from France to Stockholm, Sweden, and there he lived until when he persuaded himself again to die in 1650. He was quite persuasive to provide such beautiful analogue to death...and to his life, too. His employer, Queen Christina of Sweden, liked to start her philosophy lessons at 5.am, and so, he caught the cold and died. But, how did he come to know that he was dead when he was dead?

Perhaps he could have mused, I, myself, did die since I couldn't wake up for another of those lessons with her royal highness... Is it royal meanness? But well, his grave speaks great volumes about his death...and his existence, too. Over six months of ice covered caps, 5.am in the morning, walking on top of this ice..., this ice mountain..., this icy feeling... No, no, no, ok. It's all too wrong a premise and this story has gone dangerously so wrong. I will have to slow down the pace of my thoughts in order to think about the story..., and to think about my thoughts... Come off it fella! Enough of this philosophical unreasonableness!

We were talking of that family which I never felt I belonged to. There is also a wife in this family but I wouldn't talk about her. She is a barren desert. Ok, she has got the poise, the fantasy...pregnant beauty, and she swells. I have pulled aside a bit of her sheet cover, not to show her body here, but maybe to show the patterns on the sheet. But, the only problem is that she doesn't participate! Yet she gets eaten from the inside. And it's because she doesn't have the magical arc... She is a blind spectator watching a game she has never heard of, never conjecture, in her stupid hare-brained numbskull..., beautifully coiffures, and head. She is so boring and deathly uninteresting. Ahhh... but I am not interested in knowing what type of a creature that's eating her. You should know that. Are you interested? But death is much more interesting...

Questionings! Fears! Danger..., a dangerous thing, death is. It is so profound a thing, and for all that but for whatever purpose..., or measure, I don't know. Maybe that's why we should be happy with death.., it's the only way to realise fear creates freedom. Here we are talking about the seeds, a hazy beginning..., the future, and the start of a new life cycle. "Ha ha ha."

I wonder why they all want to go to heaven but do not want to die yet death is such an interesting idea: DEATH! But is it laughable too? D...., I want to laugh so I would have to stick to this ageing, yet so young, vocal, articulated, too-degreed head of this family. Here, I am talking of a trunk-full of them..., them papers, them degrees...
"Ha ha ha." Some white harvests with a little bit of colour here and there giving essence to this idea..., and to this idea alone.

55

He gave birth to sons, not with this wife, not with the first one but maybe alone...And there were so cruel to him; they couldn't even allow him out of the prison to go and burry his only kid who had died. So, in order to spite them, he decided to adopt the whole country as his sole child after fighting them out of his country.

"Ha ha ha he he ja..."

Just like that! His country... That's another paradox but such a ridiculous one, but could this have been possible? As if one already believes it. Talking of possibilities, talking of terrifying possibilities..., and you are talking of collecting the sun into your palms. Do I hear you saying? "You are mad!"

And my inhibited self protests silently,

It can't be done.

Really!

"Ha ha ha he he...aha."

Full hands filled with that glittering beauty..., and would you try it, yourself? Ok, just thinking of it..., dreaming about it. Doesn't much depend on what we dream in the secret of our secrecy? Wool gathering! Wool gathering through the unparalleled intricacies, nooks, crannies, storms, streams..., and labyrinth of this beautiful thought.

So engaging, so laughable too, isn't it, ah. But that's the truth, and I would have to ignore those questionings forming on the unzipped surface of my brains. I would have to say it's the truth he caused to exist, for moderation's sake, fellas. Sons he looked after, afforded some kind of enlightenment, and cultured them in the truly traditional way. I said it is the truth he caused to exist. And they were such a happy family; it's also a truth he caused to exist. I would have to allow for that too!

It now gets interesting. When those sons came off age they started being themselves and thus they started living up to what they believed in. I personally don't see anything laughable about that, do you..., yourself, I mean, as long as they maintained their identities and distinctiveness? After all, assertiveness needs no crashing but channeling. It needs fostering delicately! It can lead to fulfillment. It can lead to creation. It can lead to life and if it's tempered with, it can lead to the precipitous destroyer mentality. Assertiveness is an every minute growth..., every day growth..., every age growth..., every generation growth; it's like a cancerous growth. It is naïve and hypocritical to suppose that one could prevent such a growth.

"Ha ha ha he he..."

He is a fool. He has the soldier's mentality. He couldn't, for his life, accommodate this new extremity..., which was just an adjacent difference. Because if he were to accommodate it, it could mean those upstart youngsters were discarding to the winds of change what he had come to think of as the truth. Ok, this time I would have to delve in. I

57

would have to use my imagination and the tools of fiction to invent my own truths here.

What is the truth? What really is the truth? "Ha ha ha...." I would have to let the truth write itself then, not the other way around. As if I should know what criteria one could have used! From what perspective would one observe and pronounce something as the truth? What really is the truth? Doesn't the truth have a feminine character, like giving birth? Questions! Questions! Questions! "Ha ha ha..."

They explode! But can the truth be expressed in words? Words! Words! Words! "Ha ha ha..." Maybe that's the key. Words are a hunger to know the truth. Words name that which didn't have a name. Words scatter things into the telling like the wind to the sea's salt. Words endow power. Power! Power! Power! "Ha ha ha..."

Power begets responsibilities. Maybe that's the truth really..., the irrationalities and irresponsibility of the powerful, but what do words achieve? Confusions! Disguises! Vagaries! Aha! And everything gets pretty incomprehensible..., maybe unknown, maybe that's the truth exactly...the unknown.

But it is our minds that help us in creating the truth that we really want to embrace. "Ha ha ha..., ha ha ha- a..., ha ha ha..., he he ja."

But what is the truth, really? Dillydallying with Pilate's right to questioning, once again. Ok, I give up! Please would you offer me a dishful of water so that I could bath my paws?

"Ha ha ha..."

Pilate could built walls to protect himself from the truth..., the reality of his time, even though the mountains were singing a different tune altogether, Pilate ignored them..., the songs of those mountains..., aha-a, those songs...uu...u. I won't rein in my imaginations no, no, never! Maybe he thought that since they were still young they didn't have to have their own opinions, after all they were his blood and bones so they had to exude the same inner inspirations as his. But, is genesis effective from the inside-out or outside-in, how about the environment...and the artefacts that surround us? Is it that which we can take inside which moulds us, or it is that which we reject, or it's the workings of polarities on each other? How about our imaginations, fantasies, dreams, aspirations..., inspirations or is it beyond all these archetypal promptings. But, aren't we tool, blood and flesh, bones and will..., and we only need the word that speaks in us! Words! Words! Words! "Ha ha ha..." How is it that my teeth are already biting into my own words? So, once more, into that old old swallow...and that old refrain again!

"Baa baa black sheep, have you any wool..."

"Yes sir, yes sir, three bags full."

"One for my master, one for my Momma, one for the little boy who lives down the lane."

In the beginning there was a song and that song had words..., and with the guidance of that song's words we grew, we evolved, we separated. "Ha ha ha..." To hell with the above self-hypnosis for he has the final say on the kind of destiny they had to pursue. "Ha ha ha..."

It's just that same old line again..., the same old reasoning..., those same old justifications. I started laughing at this family-some crazy lot because whatever they were doing booted the hell out of me..., all the way, and back. "Ha ha ha..." I said all the way and back, "ha." I really had to laugh.

Not to be outdone, those young stupid opinionated ones stood by what they thought was the right thing to do. To them, there was no reason, not even a thinly plausible one they had to be puppies to their father, especially on something they had to decide on their own.

Isn't that which we are forbidden to do always so irresistible? We do things; in fact, we badly want to do them because someone is saying that we mustn't do them. Maybe it's this drive to prove these people wrong. Oftener than not we succeed where nothing else has succeeded before and thus we create new expectations for the future generations. Does this story sounds mighty familiar with what you have heard of before..., maybe..., maybe it's the same story that is making me laugh my lungs out, blowing them refreshingly out. Maybe it's the same story that is emerging from the crucible of specific political struggles. No? Maybe it's the same story emanating from all these political invectives.

"Ha ha ha..."

The father, not to give an inch to the wishes of his blood and bones..., and there goes the madness. Have you ever seen anything so funny?

"Ha ha ha he he ja urri..., ha."

He started killing his own children as if it really were that delicious an activity, like some predator on a mission not because he was hungry. Was he on a mission as such or had he gone the maddening way? He kills because he hates it. He kills because he loves it. He kills because he just breathes it. It's not a matter of consumption rather it is an act of war, not survival, no, no. He knew he either had to let them do whatever they wanted in his body, or alternatively, he had to eat them, and by so doing, eating himself in the insides.

He is now an anti-thesis to the actual function of the predator.
There is only one voice commanding him; chomp, lift, eat, eat, and it's his own voice. He is a vulture eating his own flesh, founding a garden of silence. A sad anxiety, insanity, adrenalin addiction, desire for power..., a desire for personal power..., a desire to equalize everything on a certain basic level plain and formulae. There is no mercy; a world revived by the mercy of his breath, no, there is no mercy. He just couldn't join them but rather swallow them like some mad chicken cocking open its own eggs and suckling the juice. It's his blood and bones, and the mad chicken's juice as well, and who the hell has the right to question him about that or on a lighter note, the chicken about its own eggs? All right, let's look at it this way; how could one so educated, young yet old, or is it, old yet young..., wise, educated, too degreed man, listen to his children who still have tender milky noses? They should simply shut up! How on God's green beautiful land could such a thing be heard of..., how so? Ok, it could happen in those far off strange lands but surely not in our beautiful green island. They should simply keep their cold wastelands in their own minds or to themselves, and we would keep our own warm beautiful island garden to ourselves.

No, no, no. Never ever here, no, it will never happen here.

"Not in our life time."

Surely he doesn't have to vow by his mother's name. He would surely invoke her and he would do that and you know it's a name that he would call forth with awful associations. He had promised us, never again, to call her forth from her place of eternal banishment.
Never again to inflict that kind of pain on the sea's weeds..., not his mother again, never! But, he still invokes her. And it doesn't matter that his mother was white when he was black.... No, it doesn't. He is now an aberration..., a brutal monstrosity... He is inhuman! But, it's all an abomination to him...and a beautiful thing to him, too. There; he slaughters another one and another, and another... "Ha ha ha..."

He is deaf! Deaf to the moaning cries of those he kills. Deaf to the mourning cries his henchman kills. Deaf to the silent breathings of a deviated mind and deaf to what his bitterness has become. Deaf to the anathema he has re-created. He doesn't need to listen and hear..., why would he hear it? His mother never listened to anyone and the whole country had to go to war. He doesn't even have to hurt himself by remembering. Oh, how unutterably hurtful it is to remember. Oh, how dangerous it is to listen. Oh, how unutterably beautiful it is not to think. He has made a pilgrimage into his innermost world. He doesn't want to get out anymore because it's inside where he can only find freedom.

He is now eternally trapped in his own dream state. Oh, by the way, how many will be left by the time he is through..., considering that he is still so young..., so very, very young. It's so sad.

"Ha ha ha he he ahaa...aa, ha ha ha he he ja...uuu.u.

So very funny?

Dear Zimbabweans:

Bucking the predeterminism trend
"Don't lose it before you fight for it"

J ust yesterday I was talking with my friend on the implications of the situation, now unfolding in ZANUPF party, Zimbabwe, where we see all along that ZANUPF was using the country to play its own games, to right their messy house. We also talked of the likelihood of their preferred candidate, Emerson Mnangagwa, to really embrace democracy and accept defeat when he is defeated in the upcoming elections. Will the army now accept the will of the people and let the opposition form a government? He said NO. I felt the same too. It's ZANUPF we are talking of here. My friend's reasoning doesn't stem from the fact that Mnangagwa would have been defeated. He said he would steal the elections, its business as usual, the *ZANUPuFfing* way. He said the new registration system for voters in the upcoming elections, BMV system, has already been tempered with to make ZANUPF and Mnangagwa win next year's elections. How, he has no idea of, but in his mind the ZANUPF has already stolen the elections. The opposition will not win is a predetermined thing in him.

On the same issue, my cousin feels, like a lot of Zimbabweans, it is better for us to concentrate on removing Robert Mugabe, and for Mnangagwa to take over. He says we should give Mnangagwa time, even when he knows Mnangagwa is not good for the country and will still keep the status quo, that he will steal the elections. My cousin doesn't want to think beyond removing Robert Mugabe and installing Mnangagwa. He feels Mnangagwa will all of a sudden change and will have the country at heart. He doesn't think the opposition should be given a chance to win it. It is predeterminism in him that the opposition will still fail against Mnangagwa. My question is on why we are not pushing for what we really want in Zimbabwe. Why are we accepting these as eventualities as if this is all that we can have, and be? Why are we still scared of ZANUPF, to the extent that we still give them our right to determine where we will go in life.

Zimbabweans have gone through the worst process of instilling democracy in Africa, maybe in the whole world. We have fought against one dictator for over 37 years. He was a wily, mischievous, smart, and formidable polarizing figure. No one didn't even think he will be around for over a week after the army had taken over, fighting for his presidency. The more he stayed the more he dug deeper, the more a lot of people got confused, demoralized, and gave up. After he refused to resign several times, and read one of the most wily speeches ever *"asante sanaring"* us, telling us to go to hell, the morrow day everyone begin to question the whole process, where it was going, whether it will succeed in removing Mugabe and Mugabeism.

We had doubt, doubt with doubting the process of bucking the predeterminism trend. He had to go; either through the vote of no confidence/impeachment process, the negotiation process, the election process, though I have to admit I preferred the election process, but going he has gone now through negotiations. We have lost a great chance to make it worthwhile for the country if he had left through the constitutional processes, that is impeachment and the election route, than negotiations. That way we could have jailed him later for the crimes he committed on us, and demand that he returns the money he stole from us. If we were smart enough, in the next elections, around July next year, and there was a clean sweep to power for the

65

opposition, then we could also have jailed every other thief and abuser. We could have demanded they be tried for destroying our country, for breaking and making broke the country, and this would have acted as a good lesson to those whom we would have elected to lead us tomorrow. For this status quo to continue, for ZANUPF to continue bleeding us, for us to keep failing to arrest back the country from these crooks is a complete failure on the part of the Zimbabweans and their future.

This letter is a call to every Zimbabwean out there to choose which battle to fight. They are many battles to fight in Zimbabwe now, and most of these do not get us out of our current quagmire. The first battle is to stay alive, to find food. The second battle is to fight against political expediency which the majority seems to fall for most of the times. Some had chosen their battle to be only about removing Robert Mugabe from power, only that! And these were mostly ZANUPF people and a number of political expediency undiscerning people. The others have chosen to fight the battle to install Mnangagwa into the ZANUPF and the country's political arena. And they also succeeded. Some have chosen the fight to be about the next elections, to fight to have opposition parties take over from the corrupt ZANUPF. And there are millions more who don't care who wins. They are already convinced nothing will ever change, they are losers of a fight they have no guts to even try to enter. This group consists of the largest chunk of Zimbabwean voters.

Here is a simple math to work with. Mugabe has always accumulated around 2 million plus votes in the past election times; March 2008, June 2008, July 2013, and they has been small incrementals to his tallies for the last 10 years. The MDC's Tsvangirai, at his strength in 2008 March election, got over 2 million votes too, but

66

in 2013 they went down to 1 million plus votes. It's a very simple phenomenon. Most of the voters, young voters who voted for the MDC in 2008 left the country during those tumultuous years and most never returned back. They are no longer counting to the MDC votes, if you subtract that, you see why the MDC has lost votes. Everyone knows that most of the ZANUPF voters are old people who have a deep connection with the liberation struggle, and these didn't leave the country in the last ten years more like the MDC Well of votes. The MDC and ZANUPF both together have polled around 4 million votes in the last 2 elections they competed. If you check the census on 2012, Zimbabwe has still pretty much the same population as in the last decade, meaning they were at least 2 million people who were either registered but didn't vote or who never even registered to begin with.

Usually, in any country that is politically literate, the voting numbers are more than half of the country's population, and that means our figures of voters should be around 7 million. But a lot don't bother. They are defeated even before they voted. I know for a fact in the 2013 elections, in my street, Svosve street, in Zengeza, Chitungwiza, those who were registered to vote and really voted were just a third of the total number of people eligible to vote, but they didn't bother to register let alone to vote. Ask any voter in Zimbabwe, they will attest to this. This story predominates in the whole country. This is problematic. These are people who don't care where the country will go. These are the people ZANUPF use to stay in power. ZANUPF has made the election process and voting unattractive and painful to these people, thus preempting their right to participate.

It's the same as with when a child experiences pain, he may develop different personalities in an attempt to bottle up the suffering. The pain is delegated to one of those personalities which he calls bad, so other characters can be free but neither is evil. Undoing these generations of misaligned concertized policies of the democratic process is impossible without an unshakable sense of self, a clear purpose and a lasting commitment. This country they call home has devoured them such that their personhood (agency) is misaligned with relation to spaces of competing orders. Had these people been voting, ZANUPF would be long since gone.

The connection between identity, democracy and space is purposeful, and the exploration of it (as theme, motif, and trope) is methodical in that you carefully craft your unsettled figures on both competing and complimentary spaces to engage the ever-present theme of geography and geopolitics. Place and location has the ability to devour its dwellers literally and metaphorically. In literature, space is text, a signifying theme that can be both liberating and debilitating. Once these Zimbabweans begun to see themselves as not only the owners of Zimbabwe, but also the protectors of it, they will develop a positive sense of self, and will continue to contribute to the development of the country as a whole. Thus we can spirit-rise our dreams. The experiment here is not about our root systems, but about the space between us.

Then among the people who used to vote, and still vote for the opposition, some have given up hope, some skip voting sometimes, some discourage others who want to participate, some are still confused who to choose to fight for in Zimbabwe. this is made all the more difficult by the fact that Zimbabwe has ubiquitous numbers of parties and politicians in the opposition fold, with each dreaming to be the next president; Morgan Tsvangirai, Simba Makoni, Nkosana Moyo, Ndumiso Ndabengwa, Welshman Ncube, Tendai Biti, Lovemore Madhuku, Joyce Mujuru… the list is longer. This has always made it difficult for the voters to decide which leader to vote for to remove ZANUPF. These leaders profess to be against Mugabe, but if you burrow deeper why they can't find common ground to work as one entity, you will realize they are driven by personal ambitions, ambitions to enrich themselves, ambitions to be the next Mugabe, ambitions to be kissed by the populace, and rarely ambitions to right the country.

The cult of personality has destroyed the country and Tsvangirai and Mugabe have been the high priests of this cult of personality politics in Zimbabwe. These were the drivers of this cult of personality. Mugabe is now out, but that won't stop the ZANUPF from creating another figure head, and the new cult will be built around Mnangagwa, becoming a huge clothe of red-blackened cloud that continue to shipwreck our ideal country and memories. Going forward baring illness, death or these leaders being deposed from their respective parties, Tsvangirai and Mnangagwa will be the new leaders of these camps, the opposition and the ruling party respectively. These two individuals will continue telling the story of Zimbabwe. We will see soon, when we start into the elections mode, the ZANUPF supporters will all coalesce around Mnangagwa whether they like him or not, the opposition supporters will break the opposition vote into 20 plus groups and personalities, thus Mnangagwa will win it. If we are really serious about removing ZANUPF, it's time for us as voters in the opposition, who constitute the majority of Zimbabweans, to take it into our hands and chose which battle to fight, which leader to band around, and give all our votes to whether we like or do not like him or her. It's getting clear now that for years, even though the biggest chunk of ZANUPF supporters had fallen out of love with Robert Mugabe, they were still voting him to power and that stayed ZANUPF in power. They moved beyond the personal preferences and feelings, and coalesced around one figure and have all benefited with that. They are very few people in the ZANUPF who would say they never benefited from the party through its 37 years in power.

Some got farms, some got jobs in the local authorities, central government and national organisations, some got scholarships to study, some got housing stands, some got government contracts, some got goodies like food and household stuff, some got farms and land such that hunger had taken time to translate itself into anger against Robert Mugabe. They consumed all the food they got, mismanaged the farms, destroyed the government and local authorities they lead etc, as if by accident, without desperation or a mind to conservation for tomorrow and then when hunger had settled in they folded all their fingers of blame at several of their leaders into one pointing finger against Mugabe. Then they started a fog of war against Robert.

But those in the opposition parties have fared with little and saw their country being bled out by the ZANUPF people, thus they suffered worse than their counterparts in ZANUPF. Yet the leaders in the opposition politics could always get donor funding, and abuse these for personal enrichment, and are well-off, but their supporters are poorer. But all of us have fared badly as compared to ZANUPF leaders themselves. I feel it must now stop to be about ZANUPF supporters vs. Opposition parties supporters, we all have suffered. The ideology of Us and Them among us people must end. The fences and gates cannot keep realities separate, the us/them binary fails because the two contrasting worlds are interlocked in a collective experience. We have to achieve the bifurcation of the humanist spirit together, from philosophy, ideologue, identity, economy, education, nationhood, etc... into reality, politics, science, art and poetry... We have to transcend the us/them binary thereby offering ourselves room for collective affirmation and existence beyond the control of party signifies and identity signifies like race, class, gender, sexual orientation…

In simple terms this letter serves to galvanize everyone who is against ZANUPF hegemony to work together for the better of our future. This is our country too. You don't need to have gone to war to be a citizen of a country, there is no requirement like that in our constitution. We were all born in Zimbabwe, we grew up in Zimbabwe, we have stayed in Zimbabwe, we have all built Zimbabwe, we all love Zimbabwe, maybe differently- but it's all our country. It is time to wrestle it away from those who think they won it by a gun for themselves. Let's band together and fight the new Mnangagwa cult.

At least a number of the opposition figures have put aside their differences and rose above party lines to create an alliance, the MDC alliance. Maybe the best hope we have of going forward is to go with this alliance. Let's band around this group. If over 4 million voters who do not vote for ZANUPF in every election period all vote for this alliance, then we are going to kick ZANUPF out. Its narrow minded and shallow to think Zimbabwe's problems were caused by only one man in Zimbabwe as the idea that seem to be propagating. The whole ZANUPF cabal is responsible for destroying this country. It's better for all of us who don't like ZANUPF to do this and wait for what happens after winning the elections next year, than to say the elections are already won by the ZANUPF, and wait for ZANUPF to continue to plunder our country. The army boss has said it succinctly.

In the last 5 years there was no development that happened in Zimbabwe other than ZANUPF political soaps and shenanigans. He said he is afraid of Zimbabwe degenerating into the lawless and strife torn that Somalia and the DRC have been. I know he was speaking of the security issues and the possibility of a war here, but make no mistake, with ZANUPF still leading us, we are sure going the DRC and Somalia route, only not in security issues but also economically, if we are not worse than those two countries already. It's your job and mine to see that we don't go this route. ZANUPF is not the answer to our future. It's ZANUPF we should be giving the feeling that they have lost before they even start voting. For goodness sake they had 37 years to build Zimbabwe, why do we want to give them more chances, to do what now. We are now the poorest country in the entire world, don't we feel ZANUPF has achieved enough by sentencing us to this throne.

Wake up Zimbabweans, let's have thinking hands like a musician's hands and vote for the best that gets us dancing after elections to the music of our pens. You attest to be the most literate people on the continent, but you can't seem to know how to use your education the right way. Why are the most literate people refusing to exercise their right to vote? Why are the most literate people still getting used by ZANUPF? Why the most literate people don't seem to know what the best way for the country is. Why the most literate people seem to be the most stupid and confused in Africa and the world. What literacy is that? Let's embrace political literacy and activism, let's tell every Zimbabwean who has every right to vote to go and vote. Let's decide now the way forward to our future. Let's decide what we are going to feed our families with, the schools, the roads, the water, the sanity etc... that we want for our families. When you don't vote, you condemn yourself to failure. This is your right. Exercise it.

I don't like Morgan Tsvangirai. Tendai Biti and Welshman Ncube, I don't like the MDC, but I will still vote for it. I have to position myself as a subject in a multivalent spatial matrix to measure democratic space and practice here. This merit attention; let's reorder reality at every level for ZANUPF has disrupted our understanding of personhood. The

MDC is still our best chance to remove ZANUPF. Zimbabwe politics is still about who has the best chance to represent your needs, not who we like or love. This is our democratic space. Here space denotes more than a marked room or a static enclosure; in fact space finds itself most complexly understood in time, moment and movement. Go to the elections with this attitude and win it for the country, and then we can talk of other opposition parties and the future after voting ZANUPF out. It's as simple as that. *You can see for yourself there is no N'anga (fortune teller) up my sleeves.* I leave you with this Beinsteinism....

Makudo ndemamwe angarwisana pakudya asi papfumvu anorwirana (Baboons' togetherness is that they fight each other over food but when in danger they fight together)

I am one baboon up for a fight against danger, join me!

Thank you, Ndinotenda, Ngiyabonga. No to predeterminism!

73

An Unfinished Circle

The people who owned the hand, the hand that took hold of a pen with a suffocating strong intention of making known what it wanted known, believed in and lived for. It is a pen that had the power to inscribe words of great profundity by drawing upon the piece of a paper, and on the mind of the people what no other person has been able to do.

Something akin to an awesome awakening came overwhelmingly upon and overshadowing the hand that held this pen, something that has that immeasurable existentialism associated with primordial beginnings. Something that words can never be able to fully express, it's something that resulted in the strong imaginings of a circle.

It started being drawn from an unknown place. It started being drawn from an unmapped country in the vast middle of the paper. The hand started moving, the pen started moving, and the people started moving, too. Journeying at a blistering speed like dazzling comets from an unknown galaxy, but it was to a known place. Just a stone's throw beyond those faintly glimpsed frontiers. And other things moved too..., so many things, that it seemed like everything was moving. They are a swirling speck in the middle of this indeterminate multiple blazing never ending. They are a tiny mote hurtling away toward the incredible, 'inexpressibly' expressible, never ending. A never ending demanding for a fragment grain of their questioning consciousness...a questioning consciousness that denies fear and favour. A never ending demanding for their endless efforts at maintaining their wholeness...a wholeness which is an accumulation of riff-raff, a relic of the damned, strayed, waylaid pieces. A never ending demanding that they maintained their identity...even though one might emerge from that never ending situation profoundly alien. It still is a never ending that has to be embraced!

Maybe they will change things; maybe they are changing on their own, maybe everything is happening concurrently but nothing is remaining unchanging in all this because at its most inexorable state, it remains fragmentally temporary. It is shattering, it is dissolving, and it is smouldering. It is being blown here and there. It is a small arc at one time...a little bigger one at another time. It grows, it asserts, unapologetically forward. It is an affirmation of the truth...the truth about the life this people live. It is about galling bitterness and black sorrow, chilling reality and streaming bloodshed, undying courage and unflinching endurance. It is the shaping of dreams into actions, actions into events, events into processes, processes into lives.

Lives that they must content with!

Untamed!

A people with an indomitable lion's spirit rising out of the ashes and summoning others to cooperate, and as a moving force, exerting itself in a way that no other mortal power has ever done. Thus, in its undying stance..., it confronts injustices, it confronts injuries. It confronts wounds perpetrated against its own flesh. It confronts the hard cold foreboding reality! It is a half circle. It is a half circle portraying the good and the bad, truth and lies, courage and cowardice, failures and triumphs, agony and ecstasy. It is a half circle portraying hope. Rationalization can sometimes only be valuable when it works against a mummy and action-less human background...but even at that, the bones, the spirits, the soils, the ghosts have been known to exert decisive influence on the surviving. How about when this human background can talk, coax, dictate and enforce its aptly totalitarian actions on the frustrated but still docile mass? A lot facing crisis of innumerable dimensions!

But crises are supposed to encourage us to redefine ourselves, to find steady footing to our tip tilting lives. Their prevailing conditions encourages us to show and demonstrate that endlessness within us..., that which makes us never to cower completely under defeat but rather to keep rising and rising. They keep forming us, they remould us, they keep asking for more and more, but not more than we can be able to give. After all, can death ever find all the Thomases, Johns and Gillians of this life, without running out of reckoning with time? It's not death, but life, maybe time that can be able to find all of humankind, but there is an inarguable anecdote to its endlessness. But, every ending of its every form is a beginning in itself. Every ending of its 'Now' is the beginning of another now and another..., whichever form it might really take. We have to live fully, effecting whatever changes necessary to this now, without any mitigating qualms on whatever outcome would result. We have to ride on the crest of this tide because we will never ever have a substitute of this now

It's now or...

It still is an unfinished circle.

Dear Emerson Mnangagwa:

Free and Fair Elections!

"What is your name, Skull?"

There are a couple of years at school I want to talk to you about. There is this year we got a really difficult insufferable Head boy at school. He was too strict. Even if you were friends with him, if he found you on the wrong end of the school rules, he will book you for punishment. And I had my full share of these bookings and detentions. Yes, I admit I was a difficult student. But what I also realized, even for those who were never punished by this head boy, they still didn't like him. Deep down all this insufferable strictness, he was driven by a streak of cruelty. He wallowed in cruelty. The students finally realized this about him. Even on issues where the whole student body was fighting against the administrators, he always found his side with the administrators, yet his other job was to represent the students to the powers that be. So the students ended up resenting him. The students liked his deputy who was a far better person, wished the deputy was the one on the top. This deputy treated us as adults, respectfully. But the deputy never got the chance to lead us. With the end of this head boy's term of office we selected another head boy. What the old head boy had made us feel was that office was against the students; we distrusted it, so that this new head boy took off with a student body that already despised the office he was taking over. We didn't give him time to adjust, and show us what he was all about. We distrusted him straight off. We shut him out, we resented him. And he responded exactly like the previous head boy. He punished us. He blocked us. He harassed us and we wished his deputy would get a chance to lead us. But the deputy can only become the head boy only if the head boy leaves his office during his term of office. At school that was highly unlikely, so we had to figure out a way to deal with that, and moved on with our lives.

Emerson, you are the second head boy at this school we are enrolled in for all our lives. This school has a name; Zimbabwe. Emerson you have inherited an office that we despised, that we don't like because that office was made a monster by Robert Mugabe. It is so offensive to us. Robert used that office to punish us, to kill us, to maim us, to destroy our economy and country, to make us feel like we were nobodies in our school. It's only him we had to listen to and obey. We learned to hate Robert and the office of the president. Don't be fooled into thinking we only hated Robert. We hated the whole system, the whole government. We never wished for you to take over like we wished those deputy head boys to take over at school so many moons ago. You were Robert. You are Robert. Here is a tale I want to share with you, Emerson

*****

Some time ago, not so long ago there was this man who felt he had shadows he didn't understand. He told himself there were shadows that spoke to him when he was asleep but never really grasped what they wanted him to do. And then they started to speak to him even when he was awake, when he was listening, when he wasn't listening. He heard those shadows speaking deep inside himself. The voices of which were an amalgam of light and shadows flickering, sizzling him with restlessness he didn't understand or know how to deal with. They told

78

him he had to go to a Well by the end of the village, a disused, dumped Well, where naught kids circled around the close of the day, singing, calling the old prophet to come and awash them with gold.

There is a story, a story in a story, a legend that the Well had dried in another lifetime with the death of an old prophet man of this village when he fell in this Well. It was said the prophet man had tried to retrieve a blood tree (Mubvamaropa tree) box that was full of gold. So that, even when the villagers managed to retrieve the dead body of this prophet, it was thought the Well was cursed, yet some thought a ceremony dance around this Well helped to soften the restlessness and hunger inside souls, a hunger for wealth, isn't that the only hunger that really drive us? These kids were propagating this folklore, though playfully, but in this old man the voice kept whispering to him to go to the Well. It told him that deep inside the Well there was definitely a Mubvamaropa tree box full of treasures. The voice told him to go to the Well and excavate this treasure trove.

This man, deep in his dreams left for the Well. He knew he had to listen to this voice and free himself from its restlessness. He had to go there to find wealth for himself and his people. In this night the moon was a bruise on the skies, it emitted reddish wounds of flowers of light, the whole night was in bubbles of voices beckoning, wishing him to keep going, to keep moving, and he could only obey these voices. He couldn't make himself to stop. He got to this Well in the early hours of morning. It was surreal, he searched around for the rope the people of that far off time had used to excavate the old prophet man with and he found it was still there, waiting for him like one left over log to use to light up a fire in a world with no trees. He took a small stone and threw it into the Well to measure how deep the Well was; by noting the time it took for the stone to hit the box of treasure. The thumb hit of this

79

mubvamaropa tree told him the rope was long enough to reach the bottoms. He immersed the rope with a hook attacked to its end into the Well. He felt it hit something and he felt it hook it. He started drawing it out. He felt the weight. He knew he had finally rounded up on his voices. The expectations he had for the treasures! He kept drawing it until something hang on top of the Well's mouth. It had the shape... Not of a box! He reached his hand to touch it, to see it. He was asleep so he couldn't really see it with his shut eyes, but he used his fingers to feel it, to see it. His hands closed on this object. He touches two holes on its top; and a opening below them belies a mouth. He knew it was the skull he was holding. He asks this skull,

WHAT'S YOUR NAME, SKULL? But the skull didn't answer him. He was angry and like Moses throwing the tablets on the ground in the bible, he threw it on the ground. He cried to the space above him

WHERE IS MY BOX OF WEALTH, WHY DID YOU SEND ME THIS SKULL?

Nothing answers him. He takes the skull in his hands, he looks at it again with his fingers, and he felt a song in his heart telling him it was the skull of his mentor. The skull looked familiar, like his head on his body. He touches his head, he felt he was touching his mentor's head. So he looked at the skull again and tears begun flowing down his face. The front porch of his brain knew he was himself in this skull. He was the skull. He asks the skull again, softly.

What is your name, Skull?

He only heard his own voice askance.

He took the skull and put it on his head, and it fitted him well. He knew he was the skull.

This is how we know you are the skull. It is your story's life, Emerson. Don't ask us how we came to know of this, we only know! This is how we know you are Robert. This is how we know we are dealing with Robert's skull. No, Emerson we are not going to give you time. No, I have no reason to think you will be different from your skull. Don't forget we know you were with Robert at the Well trying to excavate the box full of wealth in Marange, and that you helped him make us hate the office of the president, the government. Don't be surprised when everything you do or touch is going to create noise, anger, bitterness and displeasure with the people. What are the sounds for but to hear what isn't there. It's your voice you will be hearing.

Dear president, our apologies, we will chop you off the living skull on your head.

You are Robert Mugabe. It's you who hurt us for 37 years. It's you who destroyed the country for 37 years. The country is empty. I think if I were to go home now and knock on the Zimbabwean blue skies, I would hear the hallow sound of my own empty hands penning this missive in all that Zimbabwean blue. It's you who stole the elections for 37 years; it's you who burned down our homes, maimed people who were against you. If you think I am fibbing go to Kwekwe today and ask the people there what they think of you. Ask the Kwekwe people who burned down Blessing Chebundo's home, who killed a number of activists in Kwekwe. Emerson, it's you who killed thousands of the Matabele people. Despite the fact that you are always saying it's not you who led the genocide, ask the Matabele people who killed their families. They know it's you. The whole country knows it's you. Yes, we know they were a lot of people involved in that madness (Sidney Sekeremayi, Perence Shiri, Solomon Mujuru and the army,

81

Edson Shirihuru, Kevin Woods, Menard Muzariri, the CIO people, and you Emerson, Robert Mugabe, his deputies and cabinet, even Chiwengwa... all these are a closeted plausibility of chihauhaus, come back Joshua Nkomo!). Oh, Chiwenga can as well say what you saying too, to excuse himself since he was at the 1 Infantry Brigade in Bulawayo not the monster 5 Infantry brigade based in Kwekwe that Perence Shiri lead as they grounded down the Matebele people. Chiwengwa provided support to Shiri's 5 Brigade. You two can say you were not there when you were there, but we all know it's a lie. Even a wind takes with it evidence of where it has been. Violence is a product of systemlessness as much as a pillar of lootercracy, Emerson. Who did the target killing of the politicians and leaders of the Gukurahundi? It's the CIO. Who tried to kill Nkomo as he skirted out of the country in woman dressing, running from your thugs the CIO who were on his tail. You were the minister of security, Emerson. Tell us why Mugabe fired you, if you were not involved. Don't think we are such fools we will accept you didn't know what your subordinates like Kevin Woods were doing in the ministry you led. Don't think we are dump goats we don't know the army couldn't have done that work without the intelligence knowledge it got from the CIO. It is the CIO that helped the army extirpate the Matabele. You were the head of the organisation, you crushed them in your hands, you are covered in blood that dripped from the people to become empty shells, like testimony. So don't tell us lies, no amount of lies will ever make us think of you differently as your skull, Robert. A caterpillar out of botulism does not become a butterfly. So stop trying to persuade us you are clean, prove it. Come out clean. Tell us what really happened in Matabeleland. This experiment is to see who has been killing us, Emerson. The experiment is about a lot I don't know, the experiment is about silent things talking in the dark of now. You are Robert and the Zimbabweans have no engagement rings for you man; they can't commit themselves to a thug boss!

Emerson, it's you who killed your rivalries and Robert's rivalries in the ZANUPF power soaps we have come to expect over the years. It is you who has pushed out those who blocked your ambitions to one day succeed Robert and come to terms with your voices inside you. It's you who we blame for the killing of Solomon Mujuru, Learnmore Jongwe, the generals, the political commissars (Movern Mahachi, Elliot Manyika, Border Gezi), and everyone who was against your ambitions and your skull, Robert. It's you we blame for everything that Zimbabwe is; oh we might as well blame you for global warming! Let my pen reveal what you can't reveal to us and if I am free to speak loosely, the predator could easily be revealed. It's you who forced Robert to take farms from the whites, you who gutted the white people. Don't think you can fool us now when you say you have changed, that you now want the white people back. A crow bird, no matter how much it cleans itself, is always black. Do you know each pattern is different, like a snowflake but none is as cold as you are? It's you who pushed Robert to send our soldiers to the DRC to fight a war that has never benefited the generality of Zimbabweans, but rather depleted every foreign currency reserve the country had and pushed us into inflation. It's you who looted the DRC of its diamonds and made billions out of that Lootercracy. Ask the United Nations, they know your money was from blood diamonds you looted in the DRC and at that Well in Marange. It's you Emerson who stole elections that the opposition had won in 2008. Wasn't that you we heard who told your skull that he wasn't going anywhere, and took the whole country to ransom as you played with the work of our pens until Chiwenga's gun ruled us again? Emerson, it's you who helped create the securocratic leadership style that now subject us to poverty, it's you who re-created the monster Joint Operations Command that has run the country, de facto basis since year 2000.

It's you Emerson who took the country through a coup just a few weeks ago, and hauled your skull to the ground. You opened your big mouth which can only be described as that of a comic book character, gulped everything down at once. Didn't we hear you from foreign lands asking the skull what his name was? Didn't we hear your voice in the voice of your chummy Chiwenga asking Robert who his name was whilst his distance from our streets disagreed with us, by imprisoning Robert in his beautiful blue roof casket? With frightening speed, actions took hold of Robert in a matter of a few days. Didn't you repeatedly lie to us that it wasn't a coup, didn't you say it had no name. You called it operation restore order, you called it a coup which was not a coup, you called it capturing thieves surrounding the president, so why did you capture the skull into your hands and took it to be yours, why did you fit the skull on your head at the end of the coup. Yes, there was so much love lost between Robert and us. We had buried our love of Robert so many years ago like that village had buried the body of their prophet who had died in that Well.

But we supported you, we danced around the Well with you Emerson, and we were little children looking for something we didn't know, whittling away at the silhouette that had kept us captive so that the night of his resignation we all might sail into drinks and talk and the shared adulations of this small army of joy, the vibrations, the vibe, *buzz, bizz bizz,* the fear, and in the morning the sweepers would follow the parade march. But you hijacked that dream for us too. Even though we danced with you we knew the Well was not clean. We knew you were not clean. We supported you because we felt it was better to deal out one monster at a time. Now Robert is gone, don't think we are fools to think his Mugabeism is buried with his body, no. You have his skull on your head, Emerson. We still see the shadows. We know ZANUPF is a group of look alikes/ dress alikes/ think alikes/ looter alikes, near insanity Bono rock music look alikes who concocted to distance themselves from their boss when the people called it quits, and your ZANUPF supporters even know you are interchangeable, and that when these look alikes are kicked, other Robert Mugabe look alikes will take over like allusions of the Mussolinis eating Ethiopian checken (chicken) bones in the form of the Mengestus. You are just a new leader of an old sect. We even know you are more dangerous than Robert; that Mugabe's imaginations have hybridized into monster crops in you! Yet it's better to deal with the head of the snake than its tails that we have been doing all along. Now, you are out on the open.

We are going to fight you until you are gone too. We are on you, until we eat your footsteps in our sleep. I cast out a proud call to you Emerson; we will swallow stones, grasses, poison, bitterness, molasses, stuff our mouths with emptiness, depth and height for the next few months until the elections. Emerson, we will consume birds, beasts, locusts, monsters, fish, glue, sadza, wind clay salt, ripples…, until we become this for you, stone and only stone, until we push you out too. We know it is good to be alive, even on a leash, to test our reflexes. You are from ZANUPF. So as far as we concerned we gave you 37 years and you rundown the country. 37! 37! 37! We are not going to give you another 37 years to ruin us further. We have waited too long for uhuru, and the georgics of waiting beyond now are time as a torn cloth. We know you have nothing to offer us. We know you can only resort to buying our votes in the next 8 months or so until the elections. We see you have started the "buying us" programme. You think it impresses us that you have refused to use Robert's chariot of fire, the limousine, gold plated with the black gold of the blood he bleed from us over the years as he paraded and cocked all over our roads. Of course your emergence demand a makeover that would seem to impart change, simplicity and maturity, perhaps a whiff of Africa's present darling, a magufulication! If you think it impresses us you cut back your congress expenditure from 8 mil to 2 mil. If you think we have bought into those promises you made that you are now born again and should be absolved for killings you did under Robert, and that you now want the white people back, now that you have the crown, making it seem as if it was Mugabe only who was wrong all along. If you wanted this done you should have done it yesterday. Everyone knows Mugabe was against farm invasions, tried to fight you and the goons to leave the farms. If you think we can easily buy into this fluffy thing that you now want to compensate the whites for taking their farms forcefully, with what money, Emerson. I will come to that later (letter). If you want it done right now put pride aside man, and tell us the truth and pray to space. Achieve a better form of purity, Emerson! If you think we have bought into your lies that you now want to resuscitate the economy you destroyed, that you have started by cutting down the number of ministries in your government, and if I may ask you, why is there some process toward militarizing the government. This unassembled cabinet that is waiting for its own loot in this mineral rich country! I might come back to that, no promises.

Emerson, just know that all that you have done or purporting you will do doesn't impress us. First thing first, Emerson!

We have an election next year. Make that right, first of all. Give us a free and fair election. Win or lose it fairly, then if you win fairly we will start trusting your good intentions. Rest awhile; we are not even there yet, not even with a fair election. There are sins you have to apologize and pay for, for humankind's swelling expenses. I will come to that later. Let's stay on the elections now. I said we know all these promises were to buy us into believing you now care for us as we toward the elections. Whereas your skull gave us food and agric implements, sometimes used panties to cloth up our open business, you thought you could better your skull by offering us what we have clamored for all along to fill up our flesh, thus to flesh up your skull too. I said we know you are not the deputy head boy of this school. You are Robert, the head boy!

On free and fair elections here are the areas I want you to right. Fire Rita Makarau and her gang at ZEC. We know she is the dust that clung around the skull you have in your hands. She is Robert's lapdog, she stole the 2013 election for Robert, awarding him and his party ZANUPF the two thirds majority they now have. Just think of it? How could your old decaying skull get a two thirds majority in a village that so hated the shadows of your skulls. No, she has to go. The second issue is ZEC should be totally independent, chosen by civil society institutions like the Judiciary Service Commission, or be chosen by the Parly, with equal representation of parties that constitute our Parly. Not by the executive, not by the immediate players, not by oncoming players. The Registrar General is another public office that needs to be removed from your tentacles. Let's have the Parly overseeing that one too, or the judiciary.

The next reform area is on the military and security establishment. Zimbabwe is now a blank terrain, surrounded by two armies, one wields a gun and another, a pen. We want the army off our political processes. Tell Chiwenga and his power grabbing goons to go back to the barracks. Tell those monsters to focus their energies on military issues, not political processes. We need a law that makes it clear that its treason for the army to enter our streets to temper with political process, payable by jail sentence. If they have nothing to do at the barracks, they should help in the construction of schools, clinics, roads etc. If they are tired of mooching off our taxes, if they are tired of training without a fight to engage in, export them to the world over, the world is full of strife. It would earn us foreign currency. Employ them to farm the millions of hectors that remain uncultivated every year and grow our agricultural industry and other industries. Apparently those goats are employable and there is a lot that needs to be done to build back Zimbabwe. They should leave politics to politicians, law to lawmakers and judiciary, theirs is military. We don't have a war in Zimbabwe. Nobody is killing the other in Zimbabwe. Zimbabwe has next to nothing possibility of degenerating into a war situation like Somalia which your chummy used as the cry call to enter the streets. We are civilized. We don't kill each other in Zimbabwe. This is not bloody Central or West Africa! Emerson, the military needs to be reformed, and those who have nothing to do should be retired. The heads of the military have to be retired too. We need new thinking, fresh perspectives in this organisation. We have over 30 000 active soldiers- that's too much for a country as small a Zimbabwe, a country that has no possibility of generating a war. What do we need all those soldiers for? There is nobody in the SADC region who wants to attack us, we don't even have any territorial dispute with any country in the SADC. And on top of that we have over 22 000 reserve soldiers in the form of war veterans, and these have been used to destabilize us, destroy opposition parties and make Zimbabwe ungovernable by messing with our political processes. Retire all these veterans, too. They have no use. Those who want to be politicians, let them do that on a personal level, not using our taxes to rape us further. We need a small highly technological and advanced force that focuses on their mandates in the constitution. It's no longer a game of numbers nowadays. Look at American wars of the last few years. They are winning fights without deploying a lot of soldiers on the ground. Cull this lot. We need about 15 000 soldiers for the size of Zimbabwe. Still on security reforms, the police and civil security establishment needs reforms. Their mandates are to protect the civilians and uphold the law. They should move from the police state that they are now and have made Zimbabwe to be, into a people state police. The CIO should focus on country security not politicians security, or party games that they are involved in.

The next reform area I want see done before the elections is on the media. Open up the airwaves. Licence more players in this important field. Make this "fourth organ" of state strong and independent. We need new independent broadcasters. For us to still have 1 TV station, 37 years down the line is an insult to us. For us to still have only 6 national radio stations that are all controlled by the government, one way or another is an insult. For us to have very few local community radio stations is simply bad. Open up the airwaves and leave the journalists and media people to do their jobs in a free and fair environment, not to report according to party lines. ZANUPF is not Zimbabwe. I know that because I didn't see the memo that changed Zimbabwe to be ZANUPF republic. The media's job is to serve the people not politicians. Allow free and fair reporting on the national broadcaster, give competing parties into the next year's elections a fair share of airwaves time. Leave the internet alone. Leave people to express what they think in these internet social platforms. Let the information be shared in a free and fair way. It's laughable you have a ministry that focuses on that. I wonder what flimsy ministry you are going to create next, the ministry for love!

The other reform area is on the commission that deals with constituency demarcation. The job should be given to an independent organisation, independent from your executive power mongering hands. The constituency delimitation and demarcation should be overseen by Parly or judiciary appointed organization. We know how you have used this exercise to give yourself and your party unfair advantage over opposition parties. This is how you got two thirds majority in the Parly now. How did I come to this when I am not a statistician? When I realized the impossibility of counting to infinity the millions in Zimbabwe, I have decided to vomit these numbers. It's a big flat joke to think that a city like Chitungwiza that crawls with people from every hole, over 1.5 million people, will have 5 constituencies, yet a district like Gokwe will have the equal number of constituencies. And this capital should be damned- Harare, which has plus 2 million people has not more than 20 constituencies yet provinces with fewer people than Harare have more constituencies. Don't lie to us that three major urban centers (Harare, Chitungwiza and Bulawayo) with more than 4 million people combined together would not even have a fifth of the constituencies of Zimbabwe. 4 million people is almost a third of Zimbabwe's population. Protest all you want, but there is a grain of truth in these vomits. Let the statistician illuminate this beyond mathematical doubt, if you want. We know you and your party have used this organisation to give more constituencies to rural areas that have more ZANUPF supporters than those that are predominantly opposition. Get your power mongering hands off this cake, Emerson.

The next port of call is the judiciary. I find a judiciary that legitimatizes a coup suspect. A coup is a coup, that's the only name it is known by; otherwise we might as well call it a soup. We all stumbled as we were struck in the shock of it! But a simple truth is soldiers in a constitutional democracy can only come into the streets in times of war or civil emergences, not to right a party. Chiwenga was clear why he decided to enter our streets from the beginning of it. He wanted to clean up the mess in the ZANUPF party, period. What happened later with major general SB Moyo is known as sanitizing a wrong. I have said it before ZANUPF is not a country. Why didn't he enter the streets to right the MDC when it had power problems? We have an election to sort the country, not the army. And the sick thing is if a judiciary is blind to how the law works, how are we going to have faith in such an institution like that. Chiwenga is not the commander-in-chief of Zimbabwe Defense Forces. Mugabe was the boss. So for Chiwenga to come into our streets it had to be signed off by the president. It was Mugabe who had the right to allow the soldiers to invade the streets and break down government as they did. It doesn't matter if it was for the right causes or wrong causes. It's a wrong precedent the army and courts have set. What if the same army decides, in the future, to invade the streets again without your consent and hold the country by the gun? It's dangerous to have an army that doesn't operate under the country's constitution. There is nothing legal about that coup. So we need an overhaul of our judiciary. We want them to be independent of the executive levers and authority, to be able to safeguard our constitution against the monster that invaded our streets. The military that is bend on instituting what they want on the electorate and a conniving ruling party and cowering judiciary. Make no mistake, Emerson; a day will reckon when someone in your party will use the same army to hold you at gunpoint like they did to Robert and call it a coup that is not a coup, and with a stupid judiciary like the one that has just sanitized the coup this army will remove you from power too.

The other reform area is to do with the electoral law. Let's have an independent justice body that deals with the election contestation issues. Don't forget every time there was a dispute this judiciary has just sat on the cases that the opposition had brought to the courts. None have been dealt with; some never saw a court date. It took the judiciary 5 years to the next election to not decide the 2002, and 2005 election disputes, and then the cases became null and void as another election became due. We need an election body made up of representatives of several facets of the government, country, parties, experts, civil society, NGOs, local authorities, religious groupings…, and these would decide on elections matters and do so before a president-elect is inaugurated. There is no free and fair election in subjecting the electorate to a president who has won a disputed election.

The last issue I want to touch on is of allowing observers and monitors to observe and monitor our elections. Allow all those who want to come to observe to come. Allow and protect party monitors to monitor elections without fear for their lives. We want to see an election where the opposition can be able to deploy monitors in areas like Muzarabani and Uzumba Maramba Pfungwe without fear for their lives. Without which, don't lie to us and your cohorts of ZANUPF supporters like SADC and AU that the election has been free and fair These are areas I want to see tackled before elections next year. As you can see, Emerson, it's a lot of work that needs your focus, rather than trite issues like you have refused to use the limousine crap. We know ZANUPF party is a master at deflecting people's views to buy into an illusion that things are now fine to win over their vote. Those are only trapdoors that don't get us home. Mugabe's regime was our knowledge pond: we are graduates revolting.

Code to the core, Mnangagwa you do so move, always you do so move man, to maim us, and now you do so move, you move to soothe us. We know this gimmick; we know this thing about limousine, of catching the said to be thieves around the presidency is just useless noise. You are hiding from the election reform issues, cradling to your old ways, hiding, stealing, thuggery... If you are really serious about growing Zimbabwe again, do the reforms first and give us a free and fair election for the first time. If you win as I have noted that before we will support you to the hilt as you rebuilt the country you destroyed. It's a museum of things for us to forget too, always afraid we might forget the distance we have travelled, the trouble of stopping now. Oh we can't afford to stop now. There are no stops in these roads of gravel. The angry gestures over our former authorities and current authorities in the letter are only means in the roads we are travelling in. These roads of gravel we are travelling in will lead to freedom of the constructions our dreams. We are in phases of tilling and harvesting, November's rain fire lures us to our freedoms.

We will accept you on one condition! First of all declare what you have, and how you got it. Tell us how much you looted from that Well in Marange. Everyone in your new government should do that too. If you can at least prove to us what happened to the 15 billion you found in that Mubvamaropa box in the Well in Marange, then we will believe all this noise. I said first of all pay back what you stole, show us what you benefited from through corruption, push your cabal in the ZANUPF to declare what they benefited from through corruption, and then the whole country will do likewise. Otherwise this is just a sad excuse you are using to blindfold us to steal an election with, and when you have won then you will revert back to business as usual in something that is continuous, alooter continue. Oh don't confuse democracy and alootercracy, even if they both end in –acy…no, not that! I stop it, I am subjected!

Another gimmick you have narrowed on is the land issue. You know it is an emotional issue. You have promised the white people you are going to pay them for stealing their lands. Who is going to pay for that? I never got a piece of land from that exercise, never stole land from the white people, never benefited from it, in fact the bulk of the country didn't benefit from that, why must our taxes be used to pay for what we never benefited from. Rather the exercise has made the whole country poor. Those who looted the farms must pay the white people for the loot. We are waiting for the land reform audit. Those who have more than 1 farm, must return these to the white people they displaced to loot. They are practically hundreds, if not thousands of these farms that can be returned to their rightful owners before you start making us pay for your looting. How can we Zimbabweans be made to compensate white people to allow people like Robert Mugabe, Edna Madzongwe, Shuvai Mahofa to keep more than 5 farms each, farms they are not even using. Don't forget when you arm twisted your skull to enter the farms and allow your goons to displace the white people you lied to us that you will each only get a farm, not 5, not 14 for one person. If you want to earn our respect, stop subjecting us under taxes we didn't benefit from. It's us people who have suffered from these stupid policies like the land invasion. You meted poverty on us. And we have become who we are and learned how to cry and produce material evidence of our sadness. Don't think we will be patient as you continue subjecting us to this callousness. We are wild now, we are not afraid of your tanks. Look, we are saying, "we are sad", we are hurt enough, and we won't accept more pain. You and your band of crooks benefited from the land reform, so please payback the whites from the rent you have accrued from using those farms for nearly 20 years. There is no excuse why you can't payback the white people what you stole from them. We see this for what it is. It's another election gimmick.

In the meanwhile open up industry, clean up the mess you created with the indigenization programme. Chunk that law into the Robert Mugabe dustbin. Create attractive investment opportunities and environments in the country to allow industry to grow. Create free tax zones in the country. Use the Silicon Valley/ Shanghai method that has made China and the USA super rich, allow investors to invest in tax free heavens, especially companies that employ more people, thus this will cut back on unemployment rates and boast government tax base. Focus on creating solid banking structures in Zimbabwe, stabilize the currency, and control the financial sector. Clean up the mess at the mining sector; make it secure for investments and also secure our taxes from the mining sector. We can't afford to lose another 15 billion dollars. Make tourism and services industries grow. This is an easy cash cow as they are fewer investments involved to make money in this sector, than in industry, mining and agriculture. Clean up our image in the international community. This will encourage more tourists to visit. We have enough tourist attractions sites to make Zimbabwe a world class tourist destination centre.

As you can see there is a lot we want you to do before we warm up to you, and you don't have time or our patience. Of course we will tolerate you for next few months problematically; don't forget a hungry educated pen is both a gun and pen. First of all, and I repeat it, give us free and fair elections!

I think I am a no one or nation and this outrage is justified, there is no purpose of nation if it doesn't allow a frame where happiness zigzags with beauty.

This letter has two distinct cries. One is called *Chiduce*, an omen of good, and the other is *Huitreu*, which is extremely unfavourable! Ask Frank Herbert. Hope you have heard both cries.

Thank you, Ndinotenda, Ngiyabonga to the skull!

Doors

I
t's like you have been walking, moving. It seems in a maze of rooms, getting through passages, doors. You don't see any windows. You don't know whether it is darkness or light that surrounds you. It sometimes seems you were walking in a road, a strip road, a path but with doors. You didn't know where you were going but you couldn't stop. Sometimes you would feel as if you were walking in a road spiked with nails, but you don't feel any pain but the idea of pain. You are pain itself, so you can't feel yourself. Sometimes you feel you have been walking in a tunnel, underground, somewhere down there, but not upwards. You are walking through doors down there. You know you can feel it, you know you are seeing a particular door. It's ahead of you. It has an inscription, "this is it." You move closer and closer to this door. You take hold of the handle. You are about to open it. You are now opening it, you are opening it...

I was just thinking of a door, the idea of opening doors. A door you don't know what's lying behind it. A door that might change your life permanently, profoundly, it's a door that you know you have to get a good feel of its handle. The idea of the police detective in a crime film opening a door, in the chase of, or looking for a crime doer, who might be waiting for this police officer, behind the door, with a loaded gun. This offers another look at what that door could represent. It might be the door to the outside, to the backyard lawn, beautiful garden, and beautiful pool. It might be the door to another door, further ahead, and the idea of opening one door after another and another...it is a perpetuating feeling. It might be a door you may never be able to open. It might be a locked door. It might require breaking into. This defeats the whole image of a door. It lets that which is behind the door to take another form, posture, to disappear, to ruffle things a little, and to even change them. It is a door.

It might be a door into the very insides of things, feelings, lives, worlds; worlds that are so far into the realms beyond the scribble of this pen. This journey, into doors, the path to; it takes or asks for more, much more. It asks that you be fully there, to walk with your full weight, full feet, and full belief in the journey. To walk with the full will to open these doors and, to keep getting inside and outside of the doors. This journey doesn't require force, physical force but an inside will, a propelling will, a believing will, a questioning consciousness. It requires a great maturity, emotional maturity. It builds great emotional maturity.

I like to open doors; new doors, than closing doors, old doors. New doors propose something exciting. Closing doors is a hard take. It's either when you close a door you close yourself inside or outside the door. Closing yourself inside a door could equate to closing yourself in a personal prison, sometimes without the wherewithal to get outside. It makes you feel so caged, like you are in a prison. Closing yourself inside doors becomes a problem here, a big problem, when you know you won't get outside of those closed cells, of your own making. Failing to find answers, solutions to questions and problems is a headache, especially to problems that won't let you alone. But of course, closing yourself inside doors sometimes makes you feel so safe, secure, ensconced, protected. Closing myself outside doors tend to make me feel liberated. I feel I would rather stay outside closed doors, explore the outside world. It is a horizon world. The only problem might be that I know that I might not go back, inside the door, which I have just closed. Even though I know there is not much to be got by going back, the impossibility of it all is an idea world. This idea is an idea....

Ideas are like doors, are another thing that amazes me. They open up like doors. You have to open them, pursue them, and own them, if you can. The more you pursue them, the more you get deeper and deeper into their mysteries, their meaning worlds. The worlds of ideas can be a soft or stubborn take. Love takes to the idea of doors too. It can be a stubborn thing. It all depends on the pursuing, the opening of doors, and its own love doors. Lives, countries, worlds and many other things follow the idea of doors, the opening of doors...

Dear Constantine Chiwenga, Dear soldier: The Rule of The Pen!

We will make sure this will work, will not work, no, it will work, you will not work, simple

To keep writing about Zimbabwe is to learn to poke harder the wounds that hurt, yet you can't stop. It is equivalent to the need to hurt oneself, the need to want to cut oneself, to inflict pain on one's body in order to find worthiness in oneself. It never leaves you alone. You keep cutting yourself until all that you are left with is small pieces that can't be cut down anymore. What you are left with is nothing.

Zimbabwe defies every logic; Zimbabwe has hit every low you can think, including having the highest inflation ever on earth. Zimbabwe has charted through one of the worst terrain ever. Zimbabwe has raised more than any other African countries debates on what is correct or the right type of government. Zimbabwe has had a coup that confounded as much as it ingratiated it to the world over. Zimbabwe has been the hottest spot for fights between imperialism, corruption, racism, capitalism, democracy, human rights, poverty, governance, radicalism and many other isms as the country stubbornly created a trajectory that left its defenders and attackers all confounded and emboldened. In the middle of all this is one man: the army, precisely Constantine Chiwernga. The soldier has been the kingmaker.

I had to write you a separate letter Constantine because clearly it's you who has been involved in each and every governance problem we have had for the past 20 years or so. It's you Constantine who has wrought more on the course Zimbabwe has taken and it will be erroneous for me not to write you a letter. Dear Constantine, I know you might never get the chance to read this letter or even care enough to want to read it. If ever it gets to you. But as I have already noted Zimbabwe does not want to leave me alone. Much as I might not want to heed the pains involved in writing about Zimbabwe, I am forced to write to you to show you the pain, at least that!

Long ago, before the world had been fouled up, there was a boy who grew up believing he was special. To believe you are special is to believe in the shades of your shadows. Because he believed he was special he spends a lot of time looking at his shadows. He begins to realize his shadows was sometimes light, sometimes spotted, sometimes it had waves, sometimes smudgy, dark, darker, sometimes light, sometimes it was pitch black. And he liked it when his shadows were darker, and these he realized happened as the light of the sun faded with darkness. So in the darkness, in these dark worlds he kept entering to darken his shadows, to darken his special calling, to develop base. Thus in dark worlds he increasingly began to experience the strength of his shadows, his self. He also began to do a lot of things, a lot of wrong things to fill the dark hole his shadow was in his life. In the darkness of night he began to rob, in dark nights he began to kill, in darkness he reigned. In these killings, in these wrong thing he began to believe in himself, in his supposed specialness, and he got lost the more he delved. The darkness has a special effect of absorbing one deep and deep into itself…and the boy deepen in.

And it reminds me of Oliver Mtukudzi song about walking step by step with your shadow to find yourself. Mtukudzi went further in advising us to rather walk away from our shadows. In order to walk away from your shadow, you need to allow light to find its way to your centre, opening out your eyes to the kind of hurt you have inflicted on others as you pursued the ravishing absorbing dark of your shadows. To walk away from your shadows is to begin to realize there is a larger and better call than your specialness, your shadows. To walk away from your shadows is a difficult excursion. For a lot of people it's a difficult proposition. To walk away is to learn to refuse yourself, to learn to love something else other than you for the sake of that thing, not your sake, not for your love

Chiwenga, much as you raised up your hand a few weeks ago and waved the constitution in our faces and told us all that you were only interested in is to love Zimbabwe/Zimbabweans for its sake. Constantine to love something is to learn to deny yourself. You told us you were just following the constitution, that the constitution obliges you to get into the streets and fix up the pothole you had seen in this land you profusely said you loved. But you also decided to read the constitution of the country and interpret it, and pass a judgment as to the way forward. The questions you never asked yourself so as to deny yourself were...

Which pillar of government were you acting under to interpret the laws of the constitution? Who else, I mean pillars of government, I don't mean poles, had concurred with you? Who had the right to interpret it?

Who signed it off? What precedence you were setting? What is it you really loved?

Love drives people to do all sorts of good/bad deeds Constantine. We all see you for what you are. All you ever loved was power. All you were interested in all these years was absolute power. The constitution you were holding was the thing that you hated. It was the thing that had dented your power, so you decided to use it, by lying you loved it. There is no country to love without a constitution, Constantine. The constitution makes each and every citizen of a country feel they belong. Yet that same constitution was denying you the right to belong, the right to feel special, the right to accede to your shadows. You had to move away from it by pissing it and the country you so loved.

Your love for power has been our bane for years now, even when you were still in the shadows of others, in the dark nights you worked under to love your deepening shadows. We still felt your shadows. Constantine. You were involved in Mugabe's (your night of reveries) first fight against the democratic movements. You told the MDC and the country that the MDC will never ever rule this land. You told us you will never ever salute the MDC leaders if they were to win the elections, oh I mean erections. You and your military cabal recreated the Joint Operations Command and got involved in our elections from year 2000 upto now. Not one forgets it was you who engineered the 2008 elections interpretation, and at Josiah Tongogara Magamba base and Manyame airbase you held us and the electoral process at ransom, cooking the results to fit your purposes, that of subverting the wishes of the people. The people you now say you love and care for and that you are trying to save from that night you so loved, Mugabe. Even when your old night Mugabe tried to shine a moonlight and decided to respect the wishes of the people, you categorically told him he is not throwing out the light and give up the reins to us. You cooked the results so that the MDC wouldn't get enough to win it and form a government. You created the possibility of a run-off, which you knew you would control. And you did. You thugged us! You maimed us. Your army goons created military bases in our streets, and in these bases you and your goons beat us, killed us, raped our sisters, controlled our streets, controlled the campaigns, killed tens of opposition activists and disrupted the election. Only a crazy person could have voted in the ensuring melee. The opposition refused to participate, and its voters didn't vote. A lot of people were cowed into submission and voted for darkness. The darkness romped to victory. In an election he competed against himself, thus you made sure your adage that the opposition will never ever rule us came true. You also created a hostage president and controlled him. But everyone saw through this deceitful plan, even the usually blind SADC and AU were shamed by what you and your darkness had done but still legitimized your darkness victory by asking him to kindly work with the opposition.

Negotiations for power sharing ensured and in the dark shadows you kept invoking your shadows on the negotiators and categorically told us no security ministry was up for grabs for the opposition. Your chummy Emmerson of the JOC made sure that position was made clear to the wimps SADC, AU and Mbeki. Yes Emerson got his letter before yours, so don't worry… I told him the truth too. Morgan whom I have also written a letter, couldn't wrestle any security ministry from your darkness and settled for sharing the police (home affairs) ministry. The country entered a marriage between you and the hapless opposition. In that time of the GNU you made sure the opposition wouldn't touch your army. You refused us the reforms to make your army re-engineered and refocused back to its constitutional prerogatives. That of securing the country and its citizens against international and domestic threats against to its sovereignty. You stayed your hands in our government processes. You made it clear you don't respect the wishes of the people. You continued to weigh your guns on us as we voted in 2013 elections. We still voted afraid of your guns and your goons and what you will wrought on us if we were to choose otherwise. Your shadows decided the electoral decisions that year. Your darkness won the election. I will use the word he always uses after elections, that he had won, "a free and fair election". This term is over abused in Zimbabwe and if this word and sovereignty and integrity were to be sold like the diamonds in Marange Well we would be a very rich country. The SADC and AU wimps are the greatest abusers of that expression too, especially on Zimbabwean elections, free and fair my sovereignty and integrity to boot!

After those pronouncements the country moved on, around the circular prompts of your shadows. But what your love of power has shielded you from understanding is the country belongs to the people and you need their support, you need to make them feel they belong and thus they would work for the best of the country. But you despise these people. You think your gun is strong enough to read the riot act on the people. With so many instances you have threatened them before, by now you should know have realized a disgruntled citizen will work against its leadership. That's why you see Mugabe, despite inheriting a recovering economy in 2013 from the GNU, couldn't make headway in growing the economy. Rather the people worked against Mugabe, started dealing heavily on the black market, bastardizing several currencies, and depleting them from the country until the economy had gone into intensive care unit again. Then when you realized you are closer to the throne, you decided to enter again our political streets and used the people to do away with Mugabe, your darkness. We knew you have always wanted to lead us. We knew all this coup was for your own ends. You used the people. You allowed the people to march against your darkness, the darkness which was still holding onto the yester night of torn threads of darkness. You deposed your darkness and installed a new stooge to hold the power for you whilst you work the system until you take over.

The country is now under a military democracy with your army compatriots, the goon of gukurahundi Shiri, SB Moyo, Rujege, yourself, your puppies in the war vets, Mutsvangwa, Matemadanda etc.. being party to this military democracy. You are the real boss of these shenanigans (hahaha, a word you couldn't pronounce well when you brought out your guns blazing into the streets that afternoon on 12 November 2017), and two days later you took over our country. So now your stooge has appointed you the VP and defense minister. What more sign do you want us to look out for. You are the president. Mnangagwa is just your pawn you and your bunch of power mongering cabal in the government and security establishment will be running the show through, I mean the real show of corruption and stealing. We know you want to take over, not a day too late, and your military cabal want chances to take over after you. Our destiny is simply in your hands, not of our freewill. You are our jailer. It's an open prison, where we seem free yet enchained by our lack of a horizon to progress, we

106

will suffer more under your gun, even if we decide to choose otherwise in next year elections. You have cornered us. We are your prisoners. We have acceded to your shadows.

NB: Chinobhururuka chinomhara Constantine (everything that flies lands down). Our day will come. We will succeed. We will kowtow now to you but we will continue fighting you. We are on you!
I have nothing to thank for this letter. This pain!

Mother's Body

Children fashion out whimsicalities like "what ifs?" to deal with their existential dilemmas, and its two kinds of people who fix us to the earth: the indefatigable and the drawn-off. It's the children who fix us to a place. We are unlike children so we can't fix ourselves to a place. We are always trying to figure out our resulting identity, as a people in exile, wherever we are. To have a sense of belonging to this largest caste in the world we need the natives to exclude us and make us feel unwelcome in their countries. We have to use these imagined natives to wedge ourselves into this gap as exiles.

This piece plays on the collapsed gap between the narrative and the visual, a narrative of a life like or very close to mine. It is subjective. I am writing this with a stick on the road..., a farewell to my mother land. It is for those who dwell in dope-filled dreams of exile, imagining it to be the freedom's door. I am at the service of those who suffer from history, and humanity always creates these people. The country of our infancy dreams is now an occupied country. It is difficult to talk about the mist still rising from this land we have forgotten to hate.

We leave our country because we wanted to leave, and the second reason why we leave our countries could be a corollary of the reason why we had left it, in the first place. It's because of the situation in our mother country that has forced us to leave. Our life in our mother country was a miniature living hell. For both reasons of leaving; it is like a tot in the mother's womb. We leave our mother's womb because we want to leave, or because our mothers want us to leave and have forced us to leave. Cutting the umbilical cord when the child is born is separation in the physical sense. It's the first cutting out of the connection between mother and child.

We can also decide to cut any connection we have had with the country of our birth. We do not want to know; what's been happening there anymore, because maybe, we are busy ingratiating ourselves with our new country. Maybe we do not want to think of the painful situation we have left behind.

To stay in a foreign land is not to really belong, yet a sense of belonging grows, season by season, year by year. Staying in South Africa for me has been as if I was trapped in a car, travelling in a land I had never seen before. A land I could not touch, but I was touched by the land. On this journey, I have been totally alone and my interactions with the other people could rarely be categorized as human.

Maybe one has decided to keep some kind of invisible connection with his or her country. This connectivity can be thick and thin. It is fragile when it is constructed from memories or feelings of an absent mother or a lost mother. The memories will be an invisible web that ensnares our feelings. They are captured by a single thread which reels in the images, of the old country, or that of the mother's body and all that it offered. It is thick when it is coloured by guilty; a sense of duty, or evil blind love for the mother's country. Such would be the love that has outlived all our sorrows. The word "mother's body" wills and bodes its own remnant to detach us from neural bliss. When it is like this it leaves a solid shadow on our psyche.

I want to think there are not a lot of countries in this world where there are no Zimbabweans in exile. The description of a wondering Jew suite us to a tee now, and the description embodies our wandering away. Mother's in Zimbabwe now tended their hands, keen and call for their children spread all over the world. There is no sound: only silence in the whole country. The children have left their nests; the children have left their mother's bodies. The grief of a whole country, mourning; the dead, the tortured and the lost, it's not easy to talk about this.

Like many purblind young people, I decided to leave my country pushed by the belief that the grass was greener the other side. As I have said, I am now committed to exile, negotiating the position of refusal and acceptance of my destiny. I have understood how difficult it was to tend a land so far away from home, with so few means and know-how. I will husband this foreign land. I will stand on the streets, with throng upon throng of other unskilled labourers. I will hear my soul on these streets lamenting, and the tilling that goes on without me? In backyard cottages, shack towns, underground railways, I will lie low with my new life, wife, and children like the cactus in the sand. I will learn new customs and languages with the police sirens for dreams. With nowhere else to go, misery is when I know I can't run away from where I am because there is nowhere else to run to. I can't go back. I can't go further. I am stuck here, for better for worse.

This is what we have to deal with once we leave our countries or our mother's bodies at birth. For us to negotiate ourselves through a world that is outside of our mother's bodies, we have to learn the language of use outside our mother's bodies. Learning the native's language in a land of exile equals a young child learning his first language for him or her to be able to communicate with the world outside mother's body. The more the language is difficult and complex- the more they are many languages to learn- the more difficult and confusing the situation would be. Words (the language) become mother's body. We are formed through discourse and words are the oil that lubricates this discourse. It is also a sea of shifting valences. They are no easy interpretive mechanisms that mediate or contextualise how subjectivity forms throughout this discourse.

It reminds me of John 1 vs.1, in the Bible. "In the beginning there was word and the word was with God, and the word was God." So it means; we are all after-word(s). We are after-mother's presence. Mother is now the word, tongue, language, and the body. Separation from the mother's body, separation from our mother country, languages, and customs is the beginning of exile. At birth we start the exile so to our knowledge we have always been in exile. We are narrators, we have a story to tell, and we are the story. From our first day on the earth, we negotiate what in the past we had lost. We call out to the lost one (mother's body) to find the lost one (ourselves). That's the pleasure of our lives, and of life in exile. To replace mother's body, gender, and sexuality we exchange this with gender, sexuality and body of words; making a mother out of words. Maybe that's why it wrecks some very bad feelings and emotions when someone insults one's mothers' body.

I have now been in exile for over two years. It has been so painful, but the pain can be blunted by dreaming of the past time and space in which fragments of memories can be made whole. I go for the memories like a hungry wolf going for blood. Like the wolf, it's not uncommon to feel a shift of identity, and its fine to talk to my inside organs. It's alright to try to figure out if they still understand me, but my body has no place of its own in my new country. It seems; my body has been consuming me. I don't find enough blood or flesh in these memories but fragments of faded memories and, more dancing shadows the more I have stayed away from home. There is nothing more that must be wasted. I would have to cherish my memories and keep my blade near my centre for the sake of memory! Home now is a place in my heart and memories. The childhood home has become immemorial and recollected time. Memory and imaginations shapes it. There is a fine line that divides memories and imaginations, and in my dreams, it is so beautiful to drift and float in between.

But, as you stay a lot longer in exiled land you develop exile gaps with your mother country. You become like a fish that has been grounded on the beach. Beyond happiness or joy here, this country has simply wiped you. You are now a whistle far from yourself. It is so artificial. It would seem like you were not even there when the country plucked you out. Now this country is too huge for you to hold a memory of it, but it holds you. All that you have is misery, welcome into the real land of exile!

Exile is when your father and mother have become strangers to you. Exile is when strangers in your adopted land want to shun you because of your poverty but you haven't been that happy, in many a moon. You don't feel you belong anymore to any time, place or space. Recollection of memories and the preserved past history inside you do not bridge you to any particular time, especially when your history has been a painful one, and especially when the line that connects you to your mother's country is now a thin one.

There are no parallel lines, convergent or divergent lines with your past. You live in between these winding lines, in spaces of differing memories that decreases with time, distance, culture and values. Your disturbed wandering and tainted mind grapples and grasps for memories, like shadows disappearing and reappearing on the walls of your mind. The touch that once connected you to your mother; you know even if you were to develop that touch again, it would never make you see your mother again in your memories. You know it's enough with this history because this history would simply bind you to a non-place, leaving you with nothing. You also know that if you continue being fixed, or fixated with your history, it would asphyxiate you. You have to leave all that and start anew and that's all that's left for you to do. The past now equates to a vanished history for you.

You can't wait for this to be over: a stage, that's what you call it. When this happens, it indicates that historic memory has gone and this generates multitudes of other long term problems: of rotting love, broken dreams, and hatred of the mother's body.

Dear Nelson Chamisa: Stop the Lies

I have needed time to understand you a bit more before I write to you, but now I feel I can address you. I have been following you for years, but more intensely for the past few years. I think I got more interested in you when you used a twitter message to install yourself into the hot seat of Zimbabwe opposition politics. Seriously how are we supposed to accept someone who is dying, barely alive could find time to tweet on his twitter you to the presidency, just like that! You became MDC presidency. Since I had written a letter to Morgan Tsvangirai, late last year (2018) around the upcoming elections, the gist of that letter still applies to you now. As I noted in the letter to Morgan Tsvangirai, that even though I don't (didn't) like him anymore, I would still support him over ZANUPF, the same applies to you. The fact is even if the MDC is to forward a dog to run as its face for the elections, I will still vote for that dog. That dog is still better than ZANUPF.

Dear Nelson, oh I am not addressing Nelson Mandela. I know you might be feeling you are that Nelson Mandela. We know you are good at exaggerating things. Remember some months ago you lied to us of getting endorsements from Joshua Nkomo. Come back Josh! Come back Nelson. But nelson you are a shameless liar. You lied you were appointed to the MDC presidency by a comatose Morgan through a twitter message. Hey you doctors, dear Nelson has a cure for communication with a comatose person. Dr Nelson, can I say that...you are an ambitious liar. It reminds me of a brother whom when we were young would lie, totally lie about pretty much everything. He would tell tall tales of his greatness. Nothing was impossible to him. If it was a girl he would simply create a story of their dating, colourful stories that would dissuade any suitor to try his luck, if it was what happened to money he had been given to pay for school fees, he would tell you how he lost it. If it was why he was failing in school he would tell of the teachers who simply were failing him because they felt threatened by his charms. Nelson, you lied in Chinhoyi, on one of your infamous rallies that you are going to build us bullet trains (Blue Trains) Bullet, here I come between Harare and Bulawayo. Just think of it, a 480 plus km journey bulleting through glades and vales, the slippery scenery bundling us to the city of Kings whilst eating meatballs and spaghetti in the beautiful cities this train would pass through. You lied you would create spaghetti roads, you really got to my heart with this. I love spaghetti, I can eat spaghetti until my intestines spaghetti my insides out. You lied you will create village airports, village airports. We would really have our Mapfurira Village airport, close our home since our home was near the fields, which of course you would definitely choose to build this village airport on. *Hello Strive, how is London. I am taking a 4pm flight to Harare from Mapfurira International Airport, wow, Strive, think of that!* Hell, we will fly to Harare in 30 or so minutes, Capital here we come. We will fly to London, Paris, New York from our rural bodings. This you said you will achieve in 10 years! *Hahahaha me likes this dream.* Even the dreamer in me doesn't get anywhere close to this when he goes into dream territory. Really! Are we talking of the same Zimbabwe that is now worth a measly 15 billion dollars GDP? And how are you going to do it, creating that from 15 billion dollars in 10 years. No ways. Yes I am a dreamer like you, yes I am ambitious, and yes it can happen, but not now!

115

Now talk about how you are going to fix our roads of damholes, now talk of how many buses you are going to buy and put onto the roads for public transport, now talk of creating good roads into the rural villages, now talk of fixing the economy, the money side of this economy, now talk of capacitating industry, now talk of improving the work conditions and payment for civilians, and the private workers. Now talk of fixing our schools, hospitals. Now talk of putting a plate of Sadza and meat (we can't do without the white one) on the table. Now talk of repairing our dreams, and let our children have the dreams you have.

Nelson you have thugged around your way in politics from your school days. Nelson you love violence. Nelson you love confrontation. Nelson you are showing us the dictator that you are. Why did you bully all the provinces in 2014 to endorse you, with the exception of Manicaland that Douglass Mwonzora defended from your clutches, and why did those provinces turned against you at the congress. You were beaten hands down by Douglas who had only been endorsed by only one province. Nelson you coerced people to support you. Nelson you use and abuse God and misuse him like those Pentecostal Magayas and his thumbtack Makandiwa. You own God and use him to stamp on others' rights to leadership. Why did your thugs tried to burn Mwonzora, Khupe and Mudzuri in your sights at the funeral of Tsvangirai. Why did your thugs tried to beat Mudzuri and Khupe several times whilst you kept mum. Why did your thugs booed your comrade in arms in your presence. Why have you captured the MDC? It is your small garden like ZANUPF was during Mugabe years, like MDC was during Morgan Tsvangirai years. It is for this reason mostly that I came to despise Tsvangirai. He is the one who appointed you back into the

MDC when the people of your party had said no to you for the secretary general post. He ignored his party's constitution just to accommodate you and prevented his VP Khupe from encroaching on his post.

You used that appointment to mean you are the chosen blue eyed boy of your party. When time came for grabbing the coveted post you striked out all your rivals, using your closeness to Tsvangirai's widow to create that twitter that promulgated you into the top. But your appointment by Tsvangirai was illegal and you never thought of making it legal, now it has come back to bite you. You are illegally occupying the position you have. The universe has now spoken for the little men who tried to fight you as you grab everything and vested your interests in the party structures. You are unbundling shameless. You are a fraud Nelson. You love power too much. And that which loves power too much power will love it in return and swallows it and make it blind of its limitations. That's why your presidency has been a blundering one. You are a soldier. Yours is to kill to win the war. You surround yourself with yes men who want to benefit from blind support of you. They don't even tell you the shoes you are trying to fit into are too big for you. They urge you on.

Dear Nelson, The Rural Vote is the Key in Zimbabwe

Dear Nelson, People, poets, essayists, academicians have tried to deal with Zimbabwe's political and electoral situation and have made a lot of suggestions on how to unseat ZANUPF, but the most obvious way to unseat the ruling party is an open secret but given scant effort by the opposition. The rural vote.

117

As a country, Zimbabwe has fought and won the biggest fight, not to disintegrate and degenerate into ceaseless civil strife that we have seen happening in every other African country. We are a strong people and love our country, whether we refuse to call it home or we do. I will hazard to say we are one of the strongest people on the continent. We can have this confrontation in the rural vote and still come out of it better. The opposition party in 2008 almost unseated ZANUPF because they had made strong inroads into the rural areas. If they had done a little bit more, channeled a little bit more, they would have won more rural votes and take the presidency

As we head towards the 2023 plebiscite and presidential vote, and as the economic problems are still raw, the push should be on winning the rural vote. Zimbabwe is over 60 percent rural. If the opposition gets a good chunk of this vote, plus the urban areas it controls then it would win.

The best course for the opposition is to find each other so that come 2023 we would have one united force pushing for the rural vote. With that intention in mind there is need to create structures, especially in the rural areas, create a war chest for the rural vote, camp into the rural areas, and push ZANUPF on its tuff. Without this rural vote the opposition will never rule Zimbabwe despite how much noise they make on twitter and social media. Going to fight the war in the rural area is changing political ideologies. Identifying with the rural vote means fighting ZANUPF in its centre and centre right area by embracing and beautify some of the issues ZANUPF have in their ideological fists. The opposition needs to reframe issues like the land reform, western imposed sanctions, developmental agendas, its relationship with the colonial west, sovereignty issues, making themselves the better narrators of some of these issues so that they win the love of the broader band of Zimbabweans especially those in the rural areas

Dear Policeman: From Police State to People State

Apoliceman who doesn't care to read you your rights when he arrests you. A policeman who doesn't care to get a warranty of arrest before they bundle you in chains. A policeman who doesn't care to respect your right to an attorney or lawyer. A policeman who will beat you up without cause. A policeman who is not afraid of tramping the constitution of a country. A policeman who is always looking for a quick buck on you. Who will arrest you for frivolous crimes just to bleed money from you. A policeman who blocks every corner street, every road, every public place, every pavement on the lookout for offenders so as to bleed them dry. A policeman who barely stays at the police station, working the roads like a prostitute. A police organization corrupt right to the top of its echelons. The Zimbabwe Republic Police fits every angle I have explored so far. And more…

Application of rule of law is taken to mean application of rule to steal. ZRP (Zimbabwe Reap you Police), my misnomer for Zimbabwe Republic Police, rather than serving the people, has bleed the people right to the bone. They have created an open police prison cell in our streets, where for you to survive in the streets you have to bride your way around it. If not they will abuse you right there in the streets, beat you up until you have given them what they want- money or, you rot in their cells. Our police harvests the streets for the coveted dollars. Zimbabwe has been a country where you can create any crime unimaginable, even killing, ask Emmer's son! But as long as you know some bigheads in police or you have the big bucks you can shut up the whole justice system with money…maybe until when the power holders want to put you in prison, some 20 years later, because you have pissed them. And that 20 years later, as long as you have the big pockets, you can still grease your way out of it.

A citizen in Zimbabwe has only one right enshrined in the constitution now: The Right to be fleeced by the police. Everything else is up to the police to play it the way they want. A police state has usurped the people's right to democracy. A police that only upholds the constitution for their ends. Zimbabwe is now a good example of a police state. There are so many people who have suffered under the excessive application of force by the Zimbabwe Reap you Police and its sister organizations like the army and CIO. Jestina Mukoko, Learnmore Jongwe (who died in police custody), Morgan Tsvangirai, Lovemore Madhuku, and many citizens during the elections periods have either been beaten up or killed by the police and some have died in the crossfire between the police and criminals like my clan brother, Bizzet Mapfurira

I still remember the news of his killing when we were at school, a few months after he had been our Accounts teacher at Nyatate sec school. He was killed a few days after his betrothal to his fiancé. The sadness it brought to everyone who knew him. Bizzet was a great guy, brother and friend. He was the sweetest of our elder brothers in our village. What it meant to us to know that the brother we had known all our lives, playing football with him in our little village, protecting us against bullies had died. He was gunned in Harare when he had just started his tertiary education at Harare Polytechnic. This has stayed with me. When the current police chief, Godwin Matanga came as the spokesperson of the police to pass their condolences, some had a mind to beat him up but were dissuaded. It doesn't matter they paid for the funeral, for it didn't bring him back to us. I hated our police force from that moment until now. I despise it for all the ills it caused us over the years. It is the same police force used by Robert Mugabe to trample on our rights to protest against him. The same police who stood by and watched as the country became ungovernable in the 2008 economic and political melee. It is the same police that allowed all the other security organs of the state to abuse us willy-nilly. It is the same police force that beat up demonstrators, the opposition politicians as they gathered to exercise their right to freedom of expression. It is the same police that cooked up charges against enemies of the rulers. Remember Cain Nkala's televised murder which was pinned on the MDC officials but couldn't hold in the court of law. It is the same police security establishment that cooked up Morgan Tsvangirai's charges of treason. That tsvangirai was conniving to kill Robert Mugabe and the endless noise that was supervised by police, the debacle of Ari Ben Manashe to Zimbabwe, and yet again the courts threw it out. It is the same force that is shameless, pliable, stupid, useless. We still have that force in Zimbabwe and it works to the whims of our present rulers. That police force needs to be reformed. Not just changing a couple of heads at the top like what happened a few months ago when they removed Augustine Chihuri and replaced him with his deputy Godwin Matanga, who by all means is just Augustine Chihuri's skull. He even thinks the police is in the best shape now. He doesn't think there is need for reforms. Best shape to bleed us dry?

2017 ZIMBABWE MILITARY COUP OVERVIEW

This was the only most likely thing to happen in Zimbabwe considering the situation we were in, it was the better devil to work with. It was obvious to everyone that Mugabe wasn't interested in leaving, actually he wanted to leave his wife in charge. Despite what he said later that he was interested in leaving it to Sydney Sekeramayi. The truth is still the Sekeremayi route was just a way to make sure her wife stayed relevant, and that she or his children would eventually take over after Sekeramayi. He was committed to creating a monarchy like many other African leaders did, the likes of Ayedema, Khama, Kenyatta, Kabila etc who have created quasi-monarchy systems whereby their sons took over after the fathers, so Grace Mugabe and Sekeramayi was the bridge to make it easy for his children to take over some day. He had done the homework, though a little too late by firing Mnangagwa from the government. He started doing the job by firing Mujuru and her coterie in 2014 preparing for the last lap to fire Mnangagwa and his coterie, then let the G40 leaders unite around Grace Mugabe take over

Not only did they want to fire Mnangagwa, they wanted to kill him. The poison was the first such attempt to do away with him, but he survived it by being whisked away fast to South Africa where its effects were immobilized before it could take him. When the poison route didn't achieve what Mugabe wanted, he fired Mnangagwa.

He consulted with Chiwenga before firing Mnangagwa which from newspapers reports Chiwenga was against, thus Chiwenga became a stumbling block. He also had to go but Mugabe was naïve to think Chiwenga will still remain uninvolved in the whole issue. Mugabe knew, and the whole country knew a coup was imminent. From several articles in newspapers I read, there had been speculation that our army was fingered in a plot to overthrow Mugabe in the CIO report which he was aware of. Maybe in order to preempt this most likely scenario he wanted to cut the head of this faction and thought Chiwenga wouldn't proceed without Mnangagwa.

When Mnangagwa was fired he went under hiding as the security apparatus were hunting him, obviously with the intent to kill him. He was protected by Chiwenga's army people and they hid him from the security details on the hunt. He tried to escape by private chartered plane but the plane was refused to land in Zimbabwe, he tried to used the road, to illegally cross the Mutare border into Mozambique, and from Mozambique to make his way to South Africa where he later stayed under protection presumably of the South African government. Of course he later was whisked from the bushes through an arranged flight that was protected by the army out of Zimbabwe to South Africa. It's obvious the Zuma Government and those in the Southern African countries knew what was happening in Zimbabwe. This can even be deciphered by their lukewarm response to the coup. They all wanted Robert Mugabe gone for some time but they couldn't remove him themselves due the brotherly relationship and Mbeki's entrenched quiet diplomacy adage.

After refusing to give his go ahead arrest of Mnangagwa Chiwenga had skipped to China under government business. It was obviously in China Chiwenga worked the final details of Mugabe's ouster, with China's approval or quiet backing. The Chinese deny this and say it was just a routine government to government meeting between our military leaders and that it had been planned well in advance. My question is what importance did this so called routine military engagement had over a country that was on the precipice. Why would a country that is dealing with a huge constitutional crisis have its top military leader abandon it at that precipitous moment to fulfill a routine mission. Diplomacy aside Chiwenga was in China most specifically for this crisis. When he returned back to Zimbabwe, Mugabe had readied the police to arrest him at the airport, but Chiwenga's deputy, Sibanda knew of this and arranged a counter Army group that overpowered the support unit police send to arrest Chiwenga. These had infiltrated the Airport security as baggage handlers. So that Chiwenga arrived in Zimbabwe, guarded by a united army and proceeded to hold his first takeover press conference. I listened to the whole speech, and he was flanked by all top military generals from both army and air force in a show of force and unity.

He read the riot act of Mugabe. He categorically told Robert he is coming for him. Of course he couched that in threats and veiled thinly diplomacy. He told Mugabe to desist from persecuting former Liberation war cadres in the ZANUPF, in fact he simply meant Mnangagwa whom Mugabe had disposed off his post. Plans were afoot to clean out Mnangagwa's coterie including the likes of Chinamasa, Mpofu, Mutsvangwa etc from the

ZANUPF. The ZANUPF machinery was busy compiling the list of all those that had to be expunged from the party. Mugabe was holding his usual cabinet meeting on Tuesday, still trying to find a way to kick out Chiwenga. But Chiwenga unlike Mnangagwa was protected by all the guns now in Harare. It didn't take more than two days after Chiwenga speech when the military invaded the streets, from the Inkomo barrack, took hold of all strategic state institutions and government buildings, especially the parliament, state house, presidential offices, the national broadcaster, airport and put Mugabe under house arrest, and started a hunt for the G40 principals, the likes of Chombo, Moyo, Kasukuwere etc. Moyo was tipped he was being hunted by his contact in the army, he abandoned home for Kasukuwere's residence where the two amid firepower from the army managed to sneak to Mugabe's residence, where they were hidden. How they got out of that residence into foreign exile is still a matter of speculation, given that one time conflicting reports suggested that they were apprehended at Mugabe's residence, but a week later we heard they were out of the country too, like Mnangagwa, and his co-deputy president Mpoko who didn't return back home when these military endevours had started from his foreign state business. He stayed in Botswana until way later when everything had calmed down when he returned back home. The other G40 leaders who skitted out or stayed away from the country during this time were the outspoken Mandi Chimene who had dressed down Mnangagwa a few months before in one of those unending rallies Mugabe was using to consolidate his powers as the ZANUPF looked toward the congress in December and the following year's elections. And also Walter Mzembi and Patrick Zhuwawo. So by

126

and large the only G40 leader they arrested was Ignatious Chombo, after a fierce fight between him and the private Israeli security team and the army, they managed to arrest his and killed most of the security team and recovered over 10 million united states dollars in his residence.

The army made its first public broadcast of the events undergoing, and General SB Moyo (now the foreign affairs and international trade minister) became the public face to the ongoing military project. He was smart and denied that the country was under military rule, he said there was no coup. He said the army is just busy arresting the criminals surrounding the presidency, and once they had finished cleaning up that everything will be fine. That Mugabe is safe and is in no harm at his home. He encouraged everyone to go on with their usual day to day activities, they promised the independence of the judiciary and parliament. So in actual fact there was no coup. Because every pillar of government was still standing. They knew if they took out any of these other pillars of government that would constitute a coup in international eyes. But, in actual fact, it was just a cleverly executed coup. There is no independence, or the pillars of the government when the executive is on the run and its head is under house arrest(protection), what judiciary would pronounce this military excursion as illegal knowing that the guns were in the streets united around the same course. What police and special security establishment would have stood up to a military that is armed to the teeth, what parliament would have stood up to the army and tell them to return to the barracks. Chiwenga was now the president from that moment on.

127

He started negotiating with Mugabe to vacate the seat which the stubborn old man refused to relinquish. As the negotiations of Mugabe's departure, Mnangagwa returned back to Zimbabwe. Knowing that his security was promised. The wimp SADC sent emissaries to get firsthand information and a handle on what was ongoing, and they became part of the negotiation team. Mugabe still refused to go for pretty much a week. People were also allowed to come into the streets to demonstrate against Mugabe. Telling him to resign. And plans were made and carried forward in ZANUPF to remove Mugabe, which they did, and in the parliament to impeach him. I will make this assertion that without the parliament uniting around the impeachment of Mugabe, Mugabe wasn't going anywhere. He knew Chiwenga and his group wouldn't touch him in the glare of the media he was now in, touching Mugabe could have constituted a clear coup. He held on until he realized he was going to be booted one way or another by a united parliament. He resigned after negotiating better terms for himself and his family. He received a hefty 10 million dollars package plus monthly payments, healthy package, travel, a couple of properties, and his private properties were not to be touched too. Mnangagwa then took over.

There are several analysis we can work with from this exercise. The opposition MDC was again caught napping and its naivety were exposed again. They were used by ZANUP to ouster Mugabe and went along with this endevour without making preconditions for their involvement. They could have demanded a number of key concessions from their ZANUPF counterparts in Parliament fro the impeachment to proceed. As I noted above Mugabe was committed to staying on if for instance a part of the parliament had stayed on with him, or the other security apparatus had stood up to the military. The only constitutional way Mugabe was going was through parliament, so the MDC knew ZANUPF didn't have a majority to execute this impeachment as most of its G40 mps had skitted out of the country and were not going to vote Mugabe out. ZANUPF could only make a majority by colluding with the MDC. Some might argue this stand-off could have precipitated into a war situation if Mugabe had held on to power, which he alluded too, later as the reason why he ultimately accepted to resign. I still think there was not enough firepower outside the military to wage a significant war against the military. A lot of police didn't have arms, so also the CIO. And those that had these were being secretly dismantled, or taken captive the army that was all over the country, erecting roadblocks to counter this possibility.

The other important lesson we can learn from this is our military is pretty much the man behind the man in our government. A leader can only lead only through their okaying. It's a group of the army and former army people in the war veterans organization, and leaders of the security sectors, which is referred to a securico military establishment (or formerly as Joint Operation Command). This group has all the powers to decide the political direction of the country. It is this group that has run the country since the group was resuscitated in the late 1990s during the beginning of Zimbabwe's current constitutional and electoral/governance problems.

It is the same group that told Mugabe he is staying after he had been trounced by Tsvangirai in 2008. It's a very strong entrenched group and it would take years and years to soften its grip on our politics. Especially now that they have also captured the presidency. Whilst during Mugabe's time they were allowed to influence from the outside. Very few of their most important leaders were in the actual government, now they are in there, with its main leaders taking over the presidency, and two others with cabinet posts, and several others with several party leadership positions, we are seeing another strong shift of the ZANUPF, maybe moving toward the Chinese model, where more and more of the space for other alternatives is being depleted.

Considering that our opposition MDC has time after time failed to deal with the ZANUPF and were used and dumped time and again, and also as ZANUPF, especially its leader, Mnangagwa, seemed committed to chunk off the middle ground from the MDC as Mnangagwa collate all the middle ground into his rightist ZANUPF centre by appointing several middle ground politicians into his cabinet, into his advisory bodies, as ambassadors, the MDC is being forced into the far left or to collude with Mnangagwa, to create what Takura Zhangazha in his blog noted as *Establishment Politics*, not new dispensation politics. What we are seeing is a death of space for the alternative third agency in Zimbabwe. This is sad because we really have a huge third alternative voters block that a new party could have pre-empted to create a force to dislodge either the MDC or ZANUPF.

The truth is the majority of Zimbabwean are not party people. Both the MDC and ZANUPF has just a million members each, to make it 2 million, but our voters roll has over 5 million voters. As can be seen from that more of our voters are not really interested in these parties but are forced to choose these because the third alternative party is lacking. As I tried to investigate this in

Zimbabwe: The Urgency of Now...there are no attractive alternatives really in our political landscape. A lot of people who could have worked are spoiled with dirty from previous involvement in these two parties, and a few who might work like Strive Masiyiwa are not interested in this polarized political situation we are in.

Strengthening the "Fourth Organ" of the State

A few weeks ago, I made a follow up on the review process of a couple of anthologies I had sent to a Zimbabwean journalist who is also a poet. I had published him about 4 times in the anthologies I edited. He is the one who approached me almost a year ago to send him a couple of ecopies of these anthologies to write a review, to help us promote the books. Here is our conversation abridged. I am Tindo, my app name and I have changed his name to Journalist to avoid libel. It happened on 28 November 2018

Tindo: But brother let's call a spade a spade...you are not supportive. I can understand about money. You work in a group of newspapers but not even an article about the books, none...i even gave you ecopies but still nothing...so if you an artist who has work that have been previously published in the books never bother reviewing the books, who would then? It is sad

Journalist: Will respond fully to this assertion, it's unwise to reach conclusions before hearing the accused's side. May I as well ask do I have to buy a book which I contributed to. Newspapers should get free copies coz it's our input. Have done so much writing for many people but unfortunately nobody cares thereafter, so I changed attitude coz of people

Tindo: No you don't have to buy copies....i think i made it clear i can understand about money...no one has money. But don't also forget you contributed with full knowledge of the conditions of publication...so that argument is moot. I gave you free copies.., in case you are forgetting that. Ecopies are just as good as books in the book industry

Journalist: Motivation is critical in every aspect of life, my free copies would give me energy to review

Tindo: I gave you ecopies. Are they not books?
Journalist: We publish online newspapers but have hard copies for my family to see

Tindo: But it's you who asked for ecopies to do a review
Journalist: I can simply end here till I see the hard copies and decide on my own what to do

Tindo: Haa, you talk as if you are not aware of what we are dealing with as publishers in the book industry. Why have most of the publishers stopped publishing? I have send hard copies to your group before...and several other independent newspapers...never saw any article from them...i did send an ecopy to The Herald, they did the review with a ecopy. So this demand for hard copies...that we all know are expensive to make, and then you guys don't do the reviews, is unfair. But I will rest my case. I hope I made my point clear. I understand yours even though I don't think it's fair. Good day

Journalist: Thanks. But imagine you can send books to my News group which I never saw instead of giving me directly, I also rest my case. Another tip for you, journalists in Zim write articles for those who give them something no wonder they ignored you, sad but it's the reality in our media.

He wanted me to pay him to do a review of the anthologies. It doesn't matter he is the one who had offered to do that. He expected motivation from a struggling author to do his job which he is paid for at the end of every month, which an author, or a poet will never get at the end of every monthly. He understands the literary field, he is a poet, he knows it's all but dead. Especially in Zimbabwe where unemployment is over 90% who would buy the books. But he expected to be paid. He is the symptom of a larger problem. If review journalists are demanding for bribes from authors, how about the larger establishment. Brown envelop journalism is rife in Zimbabwe. It is hard to believe what you read everyday in the newspapers because somehow most of that information was paid for to appear there. All the writers we read about in the newspapers buy space to have their books reviewed in Zimbabwe., that must also apply to politicians.

But in politics it's even worse than that. Journalists in Zimbabwe toe party lines not professional journalism ethics. Private medias, that are mostly owned by individuals who are against the entity in Harare support oppositions politicians to the hilt, whether these so called opposition parties are running their organizations democratically or not. The same applies to the public broadcaster, ZBC, it supports and publishes info to do with the ruling party, ZANUPF. It doesn't matter that it's the Zimbabwean citizens who pays for these public medias, it's the politicians who controls them. Wonder Guchu in his collection of essays The Gods Sleep Through It All, explains these groups of journalists in Zimbabwe succinctly, *The Fourth Estate in a quandary*. He grouped them into 5 groups

> The first group is made up of state media journalists; that is the Zimpapers stable while the second group consists of the so-called independent media with the third group being those who use the new media – internet journalists. The fourth group is the journalist-cum-civic worker." And the fifth is an amalgamation of all the above. "The fifth groups consist of those who openly declare their allegiance to political parties and vow to write in defence of whatever such parties say regardless of whether it helps the majority or destroys them. These are not only found in the Zimpapers stable but across the spectrum.

Guchu concludes in his essay

> We have exacerbated the Zimbabwean problem by being dishonest to the profession. We lie and panel beat issues to suit our needs. In the process, we have become activists. Our duty to inform reasonably, to act as the people's watchdogs have been discarded either for money or self-glory. While we use the word democracy, our actions do not show any democratic thinking. Yes, the Zimbabwean fourth estate is in distaste.

As I noted, we can never be sure of the real truth in Zimbabwe because the fourth estate has absconded its real duty, to inform us of the truth, to cover news in an unbiased, balanced way, and to monitor the three pillars of government so that they would continue to uphold our rights and the constitution, and will work to change our social and economic conditions. These are the issues that the fourth estate need to be recalibrated to focus on for Zimbabwe to progress and grow.

Ingrain Constitutionalism in Church and Cultural Structures

There is no doubt that the Catholic Church in Zimbabwe is the cradle of Zimbabwe's leadership. It has created and groomed many a leader and it's not mere coincidence the presidium of Zimbabwe has always had a catholic in it. The Catholic has vast institutions and leadership levels where the young and old cut their leadership teeth in. There are several vocational groups at any parish in Zimbabwe, with for example at my parish in Chitungwiza, St Agnes Zengeza at least 6 established youth groups (Holy Childhood, Agnes and Alois Guild, Simon Peter and Maria Guild, Mwoyo Musande Guild, Catholic Youth Association, and the Servers). And the adults have several groups at this parish too (Hosi yeDenga Guild, Mwoyo Musande Guild, Mbuya Anna, Sekuru Joseph, Sekuru Joaquim), and then there open groups and functional groups like, Liturgy group, Youth and Vocations, Young Adults, several Burial society groups, Catholic Commission for Justice and Peace, St Vincent De Paul, Sacred Blood, Charismatic group etc…

In all these groups there are levels of leadership as they are executives from sections, parish, deanery (for group and parish), archdiocese (or Diocese, for group and all groups) and national level (group and all groups), and then cross grouping groups. And each executive would comprise of at least 10 members (Chairman, Vice Chairman, Secretary, Vice Secretary, Treasury, Committee members (usually 3), Organizing Secretary (with 2 Vice Organizing Secretaries), and then you can add in positions like choir master, liturgy chair, promoter, and in youth groups you would also add at least 6 advisors. This leadership applies to adults groups and other groupings, and this goes all the way to the deanery, diocese, and national groups. They maybe some groupings that goes beyond national to regional and international, especially in the priests and sister/brothers groups

With all these I think one can decipher that the church over the years has invested a lot in developing leadership

But has this been effective?

A simple answer is it has really helped to create better leaders in the church and a difficult answer is there are glaring limitations too. In these groups there is a tendency of leaders acting as if they are country politicians, not as Christians. There is excessive campaigning and collusions on sectional, friendly, parish level whereby the members will band around a candidature just because they come from the same section or are friends, yet the basic teaching of the church is we should avoid favoritism. There is abject misuse of authority in some instances, unfair level playground and favouritism, I have mentioned already. Some have been a source of sharp differences and break up of these groups

Leadership in church is a rite of passage to popularity and control of the church institutions and machinery, and the leaders have been bent on using it for this specific purpose, and thus they have subjected the wills on the unwilling followers and this created resentment and sharp conflicts between the followed and followers. Some have used their positions to build careers, and thus, instead of leadership being used to further the needs of others, it has been for the single individual's creation of career paths through linkages and exposure…

Sometime in 2016 I learned one of the youth members at our church had impregnated a girl from the next church and refused to take responsibility of the baby and woman he had impregnated. What I realized this issue had been brought to priests and the leadership of the guild I was part of and they had kept it under wraps because this youth member was a popular figure at the church and had lead several groupings including the group I was in, they protected him, especially the advisors. The implicit rule of this guild is if any member impregnates or is impregnated he should immediately leave the group as the group is specifically for unmarried (virginal purity here) youths.

But the executive, the advisors and the parish priest decided to keep a blind eye on this rule because he was a popular figure. I asked the leaders why they were applying the rules partially and I couldn't get any headway as they shirked responsibility on who had made the decisions. Not only did this the youth attacked me and insulted me for raising the issue, but I was undaunted. I approached our parish priests. Despite both the priests being aware of the rules of youth groups about this issue they had decided to ignore applying the rule. One of the parish priests was so stupid to suggest that they had sided with the youth because he had impregnated a girl from another church, not one of ours, so they had to stick with one of ours.

I asked him if the God is different and he stuttered on that. They finally agreed to revisit the issue and call the leadership to deal with the issue which I realized even the top board (diocese level leaders) where he was one of the committee members of, knew about this issue, so also the youth spiritual director and also these had decided to keep a blind eye on this issue and protected the guy.

I went to see the parish priest several times over the issue and he kept vacillating and until I left Zimbabwe in 2017 for South Africa... So it meant the issue never got solved. He got away with it but the girl didn't. She had a kid she is looking after alone and he continues with being a youth at the church. If it was a girl in the same guild who had been impregnated, there was no two ways about, she would have been told to leave the group.

This youth goes a long way back breaking the guild and church rules and getting away with it because of his connection with the church's top leaders. When he was our chairman he stole money and admitted he borrowed it to cover a mishap but the money was never returned during his term, even after. When he was the deputy youth leader at the church he misused church funds from a youth outing to Mutare, and the parish tried to recover the money and never got it back. Despite all these previous records of abuse and mismanagement of church resources, his coterie of supporters always supported and protected him from censure especially an advisor who was his close confident, who time and again defended him from all these abuses.

Leaders have also used their offices to amass wealth to themselves and their families or friends. Where offers have been necessitated for the youths, its mostly the leaders who always grab these opportunities for example attending world youth celebrations annually. We have seen leaders acting as if they were Gods (god attitude function) rather than servants (servant attitude function)

Going back to the bible story of Jesus telling his disciples they have to be servants to serve his people, which he practiced during his life, where we even see on his last day on earth (Last supper) Jesus left the high table and went and cleaned the feet of his disciples. To emphasis the importance of leadership he wanted in the church, we don't really see this type of leadership in the church; in fact it's the other way around. The church teaches and has uncalculated the wrong type of leadership in the church where the leaders function as rulers of the world, not as servants.

I have seen leaders who stayed in the same positions for years on years, and the parish priest would protect them and keep them in these positions because they are friends until that priest who protected them was transferred. This is when we would witness change of leadership. The priest have also benefited from this system of over-staying. Before the Carmelites priests instituted the new system whereby the parish priest would only stay for 3 years at a parish, priests used to stay for almost all their lives at the same parish. Now they are being moved after every three years and this has improved leadership as the priests barely have time to create and impose an unchanging system.

Looking at all these through the prism of a large country. Zimbabwe has had that type of leadership too. It's the church that has created this type of leadership. So when the church criticized the likes of Robert Mugabe it was criticizing itself. Robert Mugabe was a catholic through and through, pretty much grew up at the Catholic Parish, and had surrogate fathers in the form of parish priests, so his leadership reflected the kind of leadership the church had instituted. If leaders in the church can abuse their positions when they are supposed to be leading in godly love what of country leaders?

The heart of Zimbabwe's leadership problems in constitutionalism vs majorietism. A lot of the leaders we have would trample on the constitution as long as they know they are popular with the electorate, any day. Its politics that drives governance in Zimbabwe, not constitutionalism and servantship. I think even the general people have not a great understanding of the importance of constitutionalism. This comes from the churches and culture of the country, and these are structured in a way to make the leader more valuable than the led. Until we start building a servantship leadership system in our churches we are going to continue falling prey to this kind of leadership.

I tried to focus on my own church in this article to give you the reader a large perspective on the church. It's not only in the catholic church were you see this kind of leadership, even in the Pentecostal, the evangelicals, apostolic etc. there is no difference between church leaders and country leaders. That's why politicians in Zimbabwe now use the church institutions and the bible as the most important tool to win votes. God is now a commodity, they can parcel him whichever way they want. It is the church that allowed to these politicians.

Not to talk of the abuse of the Pentecostal pastors of church resources where you find the multi-millionaires in these pastors groups. More so in Zimbabwe, this mischievousness of their gospel is god attitude or prophetship god, and all sorts of nuisance leadership. To right Zimbabwe we need to right the church too. This is where most of us learn about leadership first. Zimbabwe is over 85 percent Christian state so it's important to understand the church's influence on the politics of the day.

The other problematic issue is superimposing the rule that leaders are representatives of God and should be listened to at all times over Jesus's teaching of servantship. The leaders become some gods, it takes time to correct them as first and foremost they are thought to represent God. This is the same problem our culture has. Old people are always correct, and it's considered rude to correct an adult. Our parents are beyond reproach, the church also says they represent the God we can see. It would be way late when we triy to rectify these adults' or leaders' limitations, and it might even be a little too late. Robert Mugabe is one such example!

FALLACY OF THE OPPOSITION MDC AND DEMOCRACY IN ZIMBABWE

The MDC doesn't have a soul (propulsion ideology) other than opposing ZANU-PF, in actual fact there is nothing that really connects people to its ideology other than the overused human rights, constitution and rule of law noises. Please note I am not saying these aren't important, they are, with a soul that connects all these to the people. People in the MDC fight against ZANUPF because of bread and butter issues, but they also forget we have an educated or continuously trying to educate themselves, electorate in Zimbabwe. The people have been exposed to all sorts of knowledge from all over the world; their mind needs to be fed too. That's why poor countries like Afghanistan have these great philosophical/religious ideologies connected to their politics that they are willing to fight for, not just food. ZANUPF has always been a party of ideologies, some well-thought, some not implementable, but they use these to fight against their failure to provide the basics to the electorate, for example ideas of economic emancipation that go beyond food like land distribution, industry indigenization(one of the bad policies), national ideologies like the Bira celebrations, Independence and Heroes celebrations, and have made national events seem like they are ZANUPF ideologies or things, and the MDC have nothing to counteract these.

The next issue that lacks in MDC is strategic intent and vision. The vision should work hand and in hand with ideology outlined above. In Africa there are visions that are too superfluous and western-centric to the electorate. Human rights, constitutionalism

144

etc… are some of these when you fail to locate them within issues to do with African humanness- *ubuntuism*, respect, community, ownership. And coupled to Nelson Chamisa's last election vision of spaghetti roads and village airports, imagine a country that is 60 percent rural and you are focusing on issues solely western-centric like human rights, spaghetti roads, village airports and when the electorate checks the roads- they are broken beyond belief- how can one dream, over-dream, or day dream to cover the chasm between vision and reality. A vision should be ambitious and sound achievable too, within a foreseeable lifetime. Seriously you can't ask humanity to bank on something that might happen in 50-100 yrs. Humans are selfish and adaptive at most- it has to happen to me or to my kids for me to be more inspired by it. The MDC talk big and *hubridiotic* stuff but there is no mechanisms and implementation strategy that is put into place to win the elections especially in the rural areas. Every election period they barely hit the ground yet the ZANUPF never stops campaigning- is always on the ground especially since the economic mess-ups of pre-2008 almost accosted the ZANUP the stick to the MDC. The strategic intent to win the elections has always been MDC Achilles heels because there is always a big chasm between their reality and their vision.

The MDC doesn't even field election agents on election day in rural constituencies (50 plus constituencies in 2018) and how can a party that fails to guarantee its voters rights to vote without fear or harm be able to really go out there in the rural areas and win the hearts and minds of more voters. The MDC thinks just because people are fed up with ZANUP and every time they fail to win they accuse ZANUPF of stealing as if MDC is automatically entitled to win because ZANUPF has failed. But ZANUPF focus on important areas, the rural vote and win that vote.

People in the rural areas have different conception of what a country means versus to those in the cities and how to measure effectiveness of the leaders. ZANUPF is still getting 67percent of MPs mostly in the rural areas and there is little dispute from the MDC about that, it shows that ZANUPF still has the heart of the electorate in the rural areas- they might not like the president in some cases, but no doubt they still view the ZANUPF favorably...the president still benefits from this love and its asking a lot from the MDC's president to win the election when they can't even deny the ZANUPF two thirds parliamentary seats.

MDC has overbanked on the noise of the urban electorate, more especially on the foreign based Zimbabweans' noise and think that just because there is so much anger in the social Medias and newspapers that would translate into votes. NO. As long as the foreign vote is not allowed they can make all the noise they could and still lose. As long as millions of youths in urban areas make noise on the social Medias and never register to vote (which is the case in urban areas). The youths only begin to vote in Zimbabwe way later when there are in their 30s. Most of the youths in their twenties, or late teens are not registered to vote, and are not interested in political issues. There is nothing that translates the noise they might make into votes. This is the problem that MDC's western handlers (US, EU etc) fail to understand.

MDC has not shaken its shameful (to the chunk of the electorate) connection to western donors (which that good chunk of the country also feel have had strong hand in our problems). The dispute with the western nations started with the land issue, which the western donors took the side of the white farmer and punished Zimbabweans over this. The land is in the hands of Zimbabweans and it was an internal issue, some Zimbabweans who got the land have used the land to change their circumstances and some have failed but still have rights to the land, and its asking a lot from the voters to hate ZANUPF that gave them land that the whites were refusing with, which the western nations punished the country over through the sanctions. A country has no iron borders within, whereby you can say *oh this sanction is targeted on A, and will never affect B or C, or D,* when there is continuous linkages between A, B, C, D…. it's a stupid western argument that sanctions were targeted sanctions as if you have removed those targeted from the country and they are living their own lives away from those untargeted. I will deal with the sanction issue separately. It's precisely because of the Land issue that the West put the country under sanctions, not the now over-emphasized human rights issue (what of Kenya that kills more of its people during elections than Zimbabwe, where are the human rights sanctions, what of the tens of thousands white farmers murdered in South African farms every year (are they not humans or it's because they still own the land), what of the hundreds of Nigerians that die in their elections), does it mean the electorate in Zimbabwe is more dear to the West… The MDC people are more interested in western donor money than democracy, I will tackle this party's democracy and constitutionalism to prove this, you get the feeling the electorate in Zimbabwe that tolerate the western ideas do so for the buck but still a lot stick with ZANUPF at the ballot boxes.

Stealing the elections is another card the MDC have overused. So if elections are always stolen, according to the MDC, why bother voting, the electorate has come to this position point in Zimbabwe.

Why waste time. MDC focuses on silly examples of how elections are rigged and never come to the table with something definitive to impress the electorate on how ZANUPF rig elections. Check the 2018 elections and the noise they made and yet when they were asked for proof by the Supreme Court, they had nothing other than theories and fumbled up numbers, as I noted before they didn't even have elections agents in 50 constituencies they were disputing the vote. Instead of seeing a half full glass by pushing to win the election so that the glass will be full and thus make people have faith in the system, I am always told what I am trying to do to correct the problem will never yield the result and thus I am made to settle for a half empty glass, and do nothing. This narrative of victims mentality needs to change or we will continue wasting our time doing these elections that the MDC will reject as long as they don't win, wasting our lives in an intractable fight by keeping asking others to try to sort of our situations and thus making them worsen than they were. Since 2000, it's hard to point on the progress we have made other than nebulous things like democracy, human rights, constitutionalism etc… We are poor; poorer than we were in 1959, the MDC says since 1923…, so tell me how one would expect the electorate to continue with this fight when he is dying from hunger, from malnutrition, from lack of a horizon to grow…there is such a thing as too much. We need to refocus the struggle issue and make a new trajectory that cares about the voter more than the voted for.

This has caused us to look around the world and try to see if this democracy we have been fighting for is the only way to grow. No it is not. There is a lot of beauty you would find in countries that are far behind us democratically but have made huge stride in providing for their citizens than we have made with our democracy wars in the last

20 years…look at the likes of Rwanda, Malaysia, Singapore, China etc…most of these countries were poor than Zimbabwe in 1980, and yet some of these countries have moved from developing into developed countries and have raised millions out of poverty without practicing democracy, at least not the textbook kind of democracy Zimbabwe is bent on. A benevolent dictator or leader is finding ground in the electorate's minds and heart in Zimbabwe, even in the whole of Africa than is democracy, the western clean kind of democracy we read in the books and try to emulate. But no western nation is really practicing this kind of democracy. We have suffered all our lives and nothing seems to becoming from the MDC and the democratic fights, thus a lot of the electorate are beginning to find ZANUPF mantra of economic development more interesting

The MDC leadership problem is the most glaring of its weaknesses. I advocated in *Zimbabwe: The Urgency of Now*, for the whole opposition body to unite together for the 2013 elections, and eventually they did before the 2018 elections. But it's one thing to unite and another thing to unite under the right leadership. Before they could really unite, the MDC president Morgan Tsvangirai died and left his party, MDC-T hang in leadership struggle he had created. Overally since its formation in 1999, the MDC never really resolved its leadership problems to show the kind of democracy they wished we had that the ZANUPF wasn't offering us. The MDC constitution states categorically that a leader only serves at a position for two terms, thus Tsvangirai's term of office should have come to pass in 2007, before the 2008 election but the party ignored that and installed Tsvangirai into a lifetime of some sort presidency. They enthused you can't change a general in the middle of a war. Where we in a war. What about the constitutionalism it preaches at every drop of a hat, what of democracy. The MDC didn't resolve the leadership problem even after the GNU, and thus it broke up further with Tendai Biti and Elton Mangoma (sec gen and treasurer) outing of the MDCT and this was the second breakdown of the MDC after the 2005 schism that saw Welshman Ncube and company leaving after disputing the senator participation vote which Tsvangirai had overrode the NEC executive decision by imposing his view, and refused the party participation, even though the majority had voted for participation in the 2005 Senate elections. This new break up by Tendai Biti and Elton Mangoma saddled the party with a murky leadership top. Tsvangirai was allowed to abuse power by electing, against the constitution of the MDC, two extra vice presidents in Nelson Chamisa and Elias Mudzuri. Why he did that is still everyone's wild guess. I will narrow it down to that Thokozana Khupe, Douglas Mwonzora, Lovemore Moyo (as vice president, secretary general and national chairman respectively) posed threat to his power as the president. His top leadership were not happy with him continuing, knowing he was indecisive and wont on dictatorial tendencies, and so those were making moves to dump him, and to counter their moves, he promoted two of his dumped friends (Nelson Chamisa and Elias Mudzuri) to crowd the top leadership and make them jostle each other than focusing on him. He learned this game from Mugabe. Mugabe when faced with unrest in his party would create something to harness the energies of those plotting against him, usually by bringing back a disgraced leader and put him or her in the middle, for example Jonathan Moyo at one time. It means the top leadership would focus on each other, trying to upstage each other instead of focusing on him.

Nelson Chamisa was dumped by the MDC electorate through Tsvangirai's influence in the MDC 2014 elections when he had aligned the whole party towards voting for him for the secretary general position. Tsvangirai knowing the threat and kind of power Chamisa had created towards the 2014 MDC elections, counteracted that by pushing the party delegates to vote for Mwonzora on the sec general position.

For how can one explain why someone who had gotten a single endorsement over someone who had gotten the rest of the endorsements would upstage this one already endorsed, without someone very powerful in leadership circles stemming the tide? As for Mudzuri he had been recalled by Tsvangirai from the GNU ministerial portfolio after poor performance, back into some shoddy secretariat in the party. So these two were taken from the MDC dustbin right back to the top 3, unconstitutionally, to protect himself from or to counter Khupe, Mwonzora, Lovemore Moyo and Abednico Ncube's threat to his presidency. As a white flag, he said he promoted those to help him, but that's precisely the job of the vice presidency (Khupe) - and when he died there was confusion as to who was the rightful heir. Chamisa, the cunning politician he is exploited the party levers and groups to upstage the other two VPs, Mudzuri and Khupe, using insults, threats, beatings, threats of arson (the youths almost burned alive Khupe and Mwonzora in Buhera during Tsvangirai's burial rites), thus he roughshod over the party's constitution that was explicit that only the VP elected at congress by the people has the right to take over from the president(Khupe here), and that no other body is allowed to elect the presidency outside congress. The party would only elect a full presidency at congress. But Chamisa used the MDC National Executive Council to impose himself and help with the control of the party leadership, thus he came to power unconstitutionally just like Tsvangirai had stayed in power unconstitutionally.

Was he the right candidate for the party, the majority felt he was so they kept a blind eye on the unconstitutionality happening, fought those who tried to suggest otherwise. These faithfuls knew if they had followed the constitution and installed Khupe, it meant Khupe was going to be the face of the party in 2018 elections and afterwards until a congress was held months later. Which, in itself, was going to be a chaotic event knowing the likes of Mwonzora were already eyeing for the presidency after doing well as sec general. It was going to be difficult to remove a settled in Khupe, let alone to vest in Chamisa. The other explanation is she is a woman and Zimbabwe, frankly speaking, is a chauvinistic society and women leaders are still one hell of salt to fresh wounds of many men in Zimbabwe, let alone to the woman themselves... Funnily enough women in Zimbabwe don't really believe a fellow woman can be a good leader. Sorry for this sweeping statement, but I stand corrected. They imposed Chamisa immediately for the future.

Was he the right candidate, at least for me who has voted MDC since 1999? It's a big fat *Hell No.* I would have settled for Mwonzora, Khupe Mudzuri, or Moyo. But critically I would have settled for Mwonzora. He was the best leader they had after Biti and Welshamn left to succeed Tsvangirai. He had the full respect of the party supporters and MDC executive (Note here I am not talking of voters) and he had beaten Chamisa in the 2014 election (I say that reluctantly) to the secretary general post, beating someone who had all but won it. Chamisa, over the years has shown he is never interested in an election that he doesn't control and manipulate to

152

win. Even the later congress for the MDCA Alliance, the party created to avoid the MDC-T power struggle lawsuits was riven by manipulations. He controlled everything, was part of the organs running the election in which he was contesting, the election was run in the middle of the night, he disbarred and kicked out provincial leadership that wasn't supporting him and his choices of candidates, and cleared out those who wanted Mwonzora or Khupe, controlled the party's mouth pieces both in the party and in general media such that the traditional supporters of the MDC who preferred Mwonzora were denied the right to determine their destiny. He used the party organs including youths to threaten Mwonzora left and right, calling him names just for raising his hand to contest a party position in the so-called democratic institution, MDC, and cajoled Mwonzora to give him wide birth for Manicaland province, and he would support Mwonzora for sec general position. Note Manicaland only endorsed Chamisa when Mwonzora had folded his towel and backed Chamisa.

There was the likelihood of the previous congress, the 2014 congress repeating itself again, had Mwonzora stuck to his guns and get Manicaland endorsement and locked horns with Chamisa for presidency, all things equal...but Mwonzoera knew he had lost his supporters in the other provinces as Chamisa used party organs to clean out Mwonzora's supporters before congress. All these were happening in a party that prides itself of being constitutional, democratic etc..

Why do I still insist No to Chamisa as the right candidate for the MDC? Chamisa basically is a tactical leader. The dog you sent out to bite up and scare competition, not the dog that sits pretty and cool until the little backing Chihuahuas have petered down. He has always been the tactical leader even in student politics, MDC youth

153

structures, as MDC's organizing secretary (the sec who does the grunt level work, the one who follows instruction from the top). For me those are the suitable positions for Chamisa. He was never the strategist who has the larger story, overview, or vision. So on the top of the MDC we have a leader who has no strategic and visionary acumen. The same analysis applies to Biti, he is a barking dog too. Even though back when he got a strategic position as MDC secretary general (from the reports we heard in news medias he messed up that as he focused on barking instead of righting party structures such that by 2013 the party was so messy, had no finances for elections and he later left with party properties and finances to build his own splinter party). It was Mwonzora who cleaned that up. Then on the top MDC Alliance structures we also have Welshman Ncube who personally thinks he is the strategist for the party…but does he have the voice to be heard? Knowing he comes from Matabeleland province, a province he doesn't even seem to have a handle on. Has he proven he is a strategist during his stint with the MDC before 2005 split, and his own brand of the MDC after?

He left the MDC in 2005 over a dispute with Tsvangirai and the MDC on the senate election. As I have noted before he favoured participation to stay relevant, yet Tsvangirai's camp favoured boycott over waste of resources. But was that enough to pack your bags and go…that's what a strategists asks before giving up. In his brand of the MDC he promoted Arthur Mutambara, a robotics professor to lead the party because he felt he himself had no power to entice the predominantly Shona electorate needed to win an election. Yes this is tribal, but at the basic level was Arthur the best he could get to lead him. Arthur behaved exactly like a robot during his stint as president of MDC-N, a Welshaman Ncube controlled robot … and sometimes

Mugabe got the hang of that robot and controlled it, sometimes it was Tsvangirai who got his hands on the mouse of the computer that controlled the robot. My question is, or my answer is if you say you are a strategic leader, then you prefer putting tactical people ahead of you, every time…there is something wrong with your apposition and analogue. Here, it wasn't even a strategic gimmick, because there was no chance whatsoever that Arthur or Welshman would win the biggest chunk of the electorate and takeover. Eventually the robotics professor went back to school and Welshman found his way back into the bigger MDC tent to start new machinations. All in all the top 3 in the MDCA position is filled by tactical thinkers and leaders. And its even worse as you go down the party levers: Job Sikhala barks more than anyone in Zimbabwe, so are Calton Hwende, Fadzai Mahere, Thabita Khumalo etc) they are all tactical thinkers, maybe the exception is the woman third vice president. This is what happens when the tactical thinkers are given full reign, they control everything by extruding the strategic thinkers because they are used to working with dirty tactics to stifle any dissent; the stable strategic handlers were extruded with Mwonzora and Mudzuri.

Years after the 2018 election, we are in the 3rd year towarding to the 2023 election, they are still barking and whinnying about the stolen 2018 election instead of strategizing around 2023. So who, you can ask. Because now we have two MDCs, each saying they are the right MDC, one run by Chamisa, and the other by Mwonzora (who took over after disposing off Khupe, the acting MDC president in a shoddy congress, replicating Chamisa's congress.). As an electorate in such confusing and chaotic opposition minefield you want to see these leaders banding together for the bigger purpose, really this is not the time to be arguing about who has a bigger penis, but no

Chamisa and Mwonzora are still fighting about who has the bigger dick, so are their supporters. Chamisa was overtaken by the events of his unconstitutionality; Mwonzora doesn't inspire confidence to the die-hard young MDC camp. We are left with one and half years to the 2023 poll and there is nothing tangible, no roadmap to wining the seats back from ZANUPF. I am sure what the MDCA are focusing on is how many seats they will get versus how many the MDCT will, its Mwonzoro vs Chamisa's egos that will play out. I am sure in the beginning of this essay I was talking of Mwonzora, not Khupe, and you wondered why? The fight has always been between Mwonzora and Chamisa…this is the fight that played out, and is still playing. No tactical runners are in the rural areas because they are at the presidency, barking at each other. We are heading toward another election the MDC can only lose. It's a waste.

The MDC's top leadership are increasingly becoming obvious have never been interested in serving the people it purports to serve, but are fighting for positions on the feeding lots. They would make a bit of noise, stage poorly organized protests to hoodwink the donors, throw a few poor people to the wolves (ZANUPF controlled police and army here) and our stupid security establishment is caught with the trousers on the knees after beating up these few protestors, and the MDC will cry pell-mell over the donors medias, get a few bucks and become quiet as they fest until they are broke again and start on another donor attention grabbing gimmick, get the loot, spend it and go back to the streets again. There is now no wholesale movement towards fighting ZANUPF'S hegemony in its battle grounds. The MDC leaders are parasitic mercenaries and the electorate is left dry and hanging, every time

156

We need a third force, an alternative party, an alternative consensus that appeals across both divides, ZANUPF and MDC. We need a third force rooted in the middle, interested in serving the people, Zimbabwe…not parties, not people, not vested interests, not tribal adhesions and hangovers that both ZANUPF and MDC are wont on.

As I noted MDC can only lose 2023. To start with it is always running late to the events unfolding in Zimbabwe. It has already lost 3 years moaning about losing the 2018 election, which if they had any strategic thinkers among them, these could have told the likes of Chamisa to move on 6 months after the election, or just after losing the appeal to the Supreme Court. If you are wise enough you won't be expecting to win anything after the last law body has decided against you. It's clear to anyone with a little bit of sense that the MDC didn't do enough to win 2018, let alone to guarantee the safety of the vote, and its idiotic to expect the last court of the land to wade into political territory to gift a party over another. Anyone who understands separation of powers of the levers of government would understand it was never going to happen. To disregard an election over little or no evidence is for the court to wade into politics, to usurp the functions of other levers of government and the country will suffer from constitutional crisis rendering it ungovernable. In simple terms the MDC failed to prove ZANUPF had stolen the vote…you can allege someone has done this or that, but without proof or evidence, it's just an unfounded accusation. This is the basics of law. They couldn't event present their own V11 forms because they hadn't fielded enough monitors, or they were reckless, or deep down they knew they had no hard evidence so they resorted on twisting the Latinity in the law and make a lot of noise, just to tarnish the election. It was their own duty to have their forms, not ZEC or ZANUPF, not the courts. As I noted I don't see the MDC wining 20123 because to start with they never focus on the right issue at the right time.

As we marched toward the 2018 election, any wise strategist would have advised them they had no chance with the 2018 presidential vote. It takes time to build a leader who would stay the test of time. Chamisa was in office for less than half a year, and had even at that come to power under through a polarizing process that weakened its structures and frayed the MDC power base. I have voted for the MDC for all its existence but I wouldn't have voted for Chamisa in 2018 if I was in the country. I was angry with the way he had shit over everything to come to power. Before Tsvangirai was even buried he had started power mongering games which really goes against Ubuntu values. I am not just interested in removing ZANUP from power. I am interested in entrenching democratic values for the future generations and now I don't see the difference between MDC and ZANUPF. But ZANUPF is always trying to deceitfully portray themselves in better light and they are serious moves by ZANUPF to gobble up that middle space I noted we need a third force for.

With the land reform and Mugabe's leadership survival games the ZANUPF became far right, radically approaching the land reform, indigenization, the wrecking fights with the West over neocolonialism and sovereignty, the MDC were somewhere in the centre to centre left on our political swing and they got a lot of support from the growing educated middle class and the poor class. But ZANUP, under Mnangangwa is moving towards the centre, even sometimes pushing to the centre and centre left thereby squeezing the MDC to the left, which is a very tight space in a conservative country like

Zimbabwe. The only way the MDC can win the elections in Zimbabwe is to push back to the centre and be the heaven of all forces that distrusts ZANUPF, and the centre of a country is where the largest majority are, in the present day Zimbabwe it's the rural vote. They have to unequivocally accept some of the things ZANUPF do to win the rural vote like land reform and push these things off ZANUPF's election basket by making them a national thing not party things. That would mean winning off its white supporters and donors, but it is exactly these donors that have killed the MDC by pushing it to the radical left and west-centric.

The hardest lesson the MDC has to learn now is to have these boys graduate from being boys into being men, girls into women. They have to learn how to grow its newfound support, close to 1 000 000 new votes to propel them into power in 2023. In *Zimbabwe: The Urgency of Now*, I noted the MDC has been losing the election with pretty the same margin since 2008 and the reason is because of *Us*, its boys and girls back in post-2000 Zimbabwe who had left the country and never returned after the 2008 election. It had not got the time and spaces to build back that base by 2013. But the younger brothers we had left when we went overseas became grown up boys, our kids we left home as we went abroad to earn a living to take care of them hated ZANUPF as much as we did and by 2018 these were the new voters who pushed Chamisa into 2mill plus votes, which Tsvangirai last did in 2008. And it is these boys and girls, on one side I am alluding to. They have to keep these boys and add more before 2023, which is an impossible order as a lot of these new voters might leave before 2023.

On the other spectrum the boys are Chamisa and his leadership cahoots. They were left with a good party, its upto them to grow up to become men and women they ought to be.

Continuing with why I think it wasn't strategic for the MDC to focus all its resources in 2018 on the presidential vote. They should have tried to win the parliamentary vote, push back the ZANUPF off the two thirds majority stage, win enough seats to make it impossible for ZANUPF to do anything in Zimbabwe. The most exciting thing about Zimbabwe in 2008 was the wrestling away from the ZANUPF of Zimbabwe's parliament by Tsvangirai's MDC. In actual fact this is where the powers are. They are the ones who make the laws, who debate the constitution, who can take the president to task. Winning the president without the parliamentary vote was naïve on the part of the MDC. How can you run a country like Zimbabwe without control of the lower levers of power. Even in 2008, and post that, it was difficult for Tsvangirai to get things done, even with majority Mps, what of with just one fifth that the MDC got. With a healthy parliamentary vote we will be set for a good show on 2023 presidential vote. Now ZANUPF has two thirds majority and has been tinkering with the constitution, entrenching their interests with at one time 27 amendments …and these would pass with a two thirds majority it has. Now winning 2023 is an impossible horizon. And this is one instance they focused on the wrong fight and came to the decisional table when it was too late.

When I started writing this essay as you might have realized the MDC was still intact even though they were fighting, now they have broken and fragmented badly into two camps opposing each other as MDCT and MDCA, this after the Supreme court judgment of March 2020 that illegalized Chamisa's ascendency to power as unconstitutional. This happened after a card-carrying Gokwe north MDC member took the party to court.. whilst a lot of people if they had read this essay before the latest schism would have disagreed with me that Chamisa and his deputies are not strategic thinkers, but after the way they handled the succession issue, especially after the supreme court judgment, I think a lot can agree with me now. Chamisa missed so many chances to seal the rift and kept to his intransigency as he preached and preached, never taking a position to seal the rift or move on. He left the whole thing to pan out the way it did. He had no wet towel to douse the fires and the fires consumed him and the party. He kept making so many accusations against ZANUPF even though the drama was playing out inside the MDC, he blamed everyone else, and his supporters blamed everyone else with their *Chamisa chete chete* slogans. He is still playing the victim's game that Tsvangirai perfected and this cult of leadership has left the MDC in the open. ZANUPF has moved away from *Mugabe chete chete* mantra, at least not as publicly as they used to do. Mnangagwa's speech a few months ago shows that's where he is driving the party towards when he said the days of the spectre of leadership died with Mugabe. It needs to die too in the MDC, or just being publicly shunned in the party.

161

Screw the Zimbabwean!

From far off memory the story of Zimbabwe or Zimbabweans has been of screwing and being screwed. We love being screwed. We screw each other. If you like screwing please go to Zimbabwe. Here, it's a Zimbabwe of both black and white. The Shona people screwed the Khoi people off their land, then the Shona were screwed by the Ndebele, the Ndebele and Shona were screwed by the Whites, and these returned the favour, screwed the Whites. Blacks screwed Whites, Whites screwed Blacks, throw in the Indians, Chinese, Coloureds etc …it's a *screwing screw, screw screw zhiiim zhiim pot*. It's the sounds of the screws and drill machine, filling every hole it is holeing into. Mugabe screwed the Zimbabweans for over 37 years, and we allowed him to screw us as we moaned with pleasure. *Ummm, aaaah, ishsss….,* Please note Zimbabweans love being screwed so don't mistake the noise they make when they are being screwed by their politicians as pain. No, it's pleasure! When Mugabe was done screwing the Zimbos, he left it to his protégé to continue screwing them. Hear them now as they moan! *"There is no food", "There is no fuel", "There is no electricity", "There is no water", "There is no foreign currency", "There is not enough school fees", "There is no transport", "There are no jobs", "There is no industry", "There is no president", "There is no hope", "There is no this", "There is no that and those ones"* Even you can hear the mournful sounds in these noises. They are actually enjoying being screwed. They allowed for that. When you think you know so much, and the Zimbabweans boast about being the most educated people in Africa- I am sure you have heard of this noise- in actual fact you don't know a thing. You should be learning. You should be growing. You should be adapting. Tell me why would a people who hated what Robert did to them for 37 years, would allow the same screwer to get away with all that he stole, all the sadness and pain he visited upon them. They all agreed to leave Robert alone and let him rest. I am sure the old screwer still chuckles at the Zimbabweans with unbelief at how he got away with all that! If he was that bad he should be rotting in jail. Screw human dignity, where is the human dignity for the millions he screwed for a lifetime, screw mercies and the we-are-the-most-civilized-people-on-the-continent self-hypnosis, screw the Zimbabweans and their civilized poverty of mind and existence! This would have served as a reminder to Mnangagwa that if he screws us he will eventually face the same screws, but no, we didn't. Now Mnangagwa is happily screwing us left, right and centre and we are enjoying it. Sideways, backwards, in the mouth, every hole is filled up as the crocodile drills us. And mark my words, the next in line will come and screw us. You can go and debate who you think is the next in line but for sure he will screw us, whether it's the, *it will work*, soldier... Note: yes it will work in screwing us, or whether it's the little boycrazywarhead power gloat, screwbag of opposition politics. He so loves moaning about how Mnangagwa is screwing us whilst he is screwing us himself. So to you African brother and sister out there when you see a Zimbabwean, know that he is screwier screwable. Try to screw him. South Africa, I didn't say do xenophobia on him, just screw him. You are asking me how? It's very simple, just screw his malleable mind. And he will never let go of you! You American, Russian, Indian, Chinese, European, Asian... come to the African tropical paradise of screwing and enjoy yourself. And I tell you, the Zimbabwean will be so grateful for the screwing!

IT STIRS; IT STIRS....AND IT STIRS

He has seen much more than he could even remember. With every new turn things changed. He has come to accept that there is no absolute in life, that life in itself is not an absolute, that there is always something stirring beyond the frontiers.

New things. New trends. New beliefs. New movements. New lives.... New, new, new, new... and everything becoming a terrifying make-believe frontier district, and always something beyond these new frontier districts, coming and changing considerably..., sometimes completely, what everyone has come to believe to as the truth. That man's life is a complete inexperience..., from the tot who has just entered an alien world, a world that adults call real..., to old age that is so innocent..., completely lacking, so uninitiated in new things that have come just lately, things that they never thought of, things that thinking about their existence seemed too farfetched an idea.

Today, Sekuru isn't so sure anymore. He isn't so sure whether he still believes in the exorability of the ultimate. He isn't so sure of the ultimatum entering into its own metamorphosis unending endlessness. There also seems to be too many casualties on the sidelines as if everything has derailed off the course. Everyone else, even those who wished to be sidelined were being swallowed unwillingly or held at deathly ransom.

There is also this feeling... A feeling of trailing behind, a feeling of being left behind in the hostile wilderness as things begin to gird-up faster and faster than he is able to keep abreast. There is a fast fiery wind in the air, even in people' movements, touches, looks, gestures and postures. It is a feeling of something stirring everything to a particular movement...

It is almost end of winter and Sekuru has wandered up to the fields. Something has compelled him to undertake this journey. A thought, a feeling, maybe something that pushes us and put us on invidious positions, positions that would allow us to observe things that not everyone else would be observing.

It has been months and months ever since he has taken this kind of a walk. All along he felt he was no longer capable of such a pilgrimage. But, somehow, he has managed it, almost as easily as if it is something he did regularly. He sits a little bit, under a 'burdened with fruits' Muhacha tree, *Parinari curatellifolia*, just by the road's sides. He wants to rest his ageing bones and perhaps steal a glance at the wonderfully gentle, flowing veldts, which stretches from his feet until they glances the far-off Nyangombe River and the small patches of hills to the north.

Then, he sees a strange movement..., just a tiny blip of it. It is a very small, tiny insignificant movement. Maybe his old eyes were playing a cruel insane game with him or had he been expectantly waiting for this to happen. Such that he thought it happened yet in actual fact it hadn't occurred, maybe he is insane! It is that kind of sane insanity that goes hand in hand with senility. He really must be, now that he is so old he isn't so sure what actually tallies with serenity, or maybe...

Then, there it is, it's another tiny movement like the last tail of mist writhing out of the valley's banks under the sun's incessant pounding. It stirs; it stirs..., and it stirs... It is smoke from the burning fire started from the matchstick thrown onto the grass by the young man he has seen passing by. As the smoke starts growing, so does, in the first place, a tiny flame. It starts slowly, silently, slowly..., until it starts moving in the direction of the wind. There is something about this fire..., the way it started, its growth, and its suddenly faster and fiery movement... It is a fire that behoves a strong and strange purpose. He simply has to stir clear of it.

He takes hold of his walking stick and dashes swiftly like a young energetic man across the wide road to safety. And, he can't help musing about this magnificent spectacle; which was to find a lot of conquests in its brood, especially those that don't tune up to its prodigious movement, a movement that is intolerably too fast for the old man. It is not only this fire that makes him think about these dark sad thoughts. It is the merging panorama of warring feelings wrecking his old frame, agonizingly denying any defined form.

All the dry trees and even some green trees are burned. It burned tiny animals of the grass; ants, termites, locusts and some other bigger animals that it surrounded. Only those that can run faster and some many green trees survived from it but with visible scars to show. It speed-eagled north and south along the road, thereby covering infinite-some distances in these directions. It stirs; it stirs..., and it stirs. It is now a body..., big..., insurmountable in its deadly quest to silence everything...

To change everything; to bring a completely new picture that has fewer or no linings with the old picture.

It stirs; it stirs..., and it stirs, again and again. Beyond the valley intersecting the veldt, beyond the upland, beyond the hills, in the far off distances the smoke and fire could be seen stirring higher and higher in dark-dusty clouds of smoke thereby reddening and greying the sky to the west.

It stirs; it stirs..., and it stirs, again and again. Small patches of smoke and sometimes fire, here and there doing their outmost to totally burn out the left over logs, dry cow dung, plastic papers and many other things that withstood the fire's first scotches which were now far of the horizon.

It stirs; it stirs..., and it stirs, again and again. For the first time that morning Sekuru feels the uneasiness evaporating..., leaving a feeling of loneliness, of being left behind..., unmoving..., in his own world.

It stirs; it stirs..., and it stirs, again and again. He starts crying silently. Big rolling tears tumbling..., one after another and another...

It stirs; it stirs..., and it stirs, again and again...

Mmap Nonfiction and Academic books

If you have enjoyed *Zimbabwe: Beyond Robert Mugabe,* consider these other fine *Mmap Nonfiction and Academic* books from Mwanaka Media and Publishing:

Cultural Hybridity and Fixity by Andrew Nyongesa
Tintinnabulation of Literary Theory by Andrew Nyongesa
South Africa and United Nations Peacekeeping Offensive Operations by Antonio Garcia
A Case of Love and Hate by Chenjerai Mhondera
A Cat and Mouse Affair by Bruno Shora
The Scholarship Girl by Abigail George
The Gods Sleep Through It All by Wonder Guchu
PHENOMENOLOGY OF DECOLONIZING THE UNIVERSITY: *Essays in the Contemporary Thoughts of Afrikology* by Zvikomborero Kapuya
Africanization and Americanization Anthology Volume 1, Searching for Interracial, Interstitial, Intersectional and Interstates Meeting Spaces, Africa Vs North America by Tendai R Mwanaka
Africa, UK and Ireland: Writing Politics and Knowledge Production Vol 1 by Tendai R Mwanaka
Writing Language, Culture and Development, Africa Vs Asia Vol 1 by Tendai R Mwanaka, Wanjohi wa Makokha and Upal Deb
Zimbolicious: An Anthology of Zimbabwean Literature and Arts, Vol 3 by Tendai Mwanaka
Drawing Without Licence by Tendai R Mwanaka
Writing Grandmothers/ Escribiendo sobre nuestras raíces: Africa Vs Latin America Vol 2 by Tendai R Mwanaka and Felix Rodriguez

Nationalism: (Mis)Understanding Donald Trump's Capitalism, Racism, Global Politics, International Trade and Media Wars, Africa Vs North America Vol 2 by Tendai R Mwanaka

It Is Not About Me: Diaries 2010-2011 by Tendai Rinos Mwanaka

Chitungwiza Mushamukuru: An Anthology from Zimbabwe's Biggest Ghetto Town by Tendai Rinos Mwanaka

The Day and the Dweller: A Study of the Emerald Tablets by Jonathan Thompson

Zimbolicious Anthology Vol 4: An Anthology of Zimbabwean Literature and Arts by Tendai Rinos Mwanaka and Jabulani Mzinyathi

Parks and Recreation by Abigail George

FAMILY LAW AND POLITICS WITH BIOLOGY AND ROYALTY IN AFRICA AND NORTH AMERICA by Peter Ateh-Afec Fossungo

Writing Robotics, Africa Vs Asia, Vol 2 by Tendai Rinos Mwanaka

Zimbolicious Anthology Vol 5: An Anthology of Zimbabwean Literature and Arts by Tendai R. Mwanaka

Love Notes: Everything is Love, An Anthology of Indigenous Languages of Africa and East Europe by Tendai R Mwanaka

Zimbolicious Anthology Vol 6: An Anthology of Zimbabwean Literature and Arts by Tendai R. Mwanaka and Chenjerai Mhondera

BATTLING LANGUAGE RIGHTS GOVERNANCE IN AFRICA: SWISSELGIANISM, UBACKISM, AND THE AMBAZONIA-CAMEROUN WAR by Peter Ateh-Afec Fossungo

Otherness and Pathology: The Fragmented Self and Madness in Contemporary African Fiction by Andrew Nyongesa

Upcoming

Zimbabwe: The Blame Game, New and Recollected essays and Non-fictions by Tendai Rinos Mwanaka

The Trick is to Keep Breathing: Covid 19 Stories From African and North American Writers, Vol 3 by Tendai Rinos Mwanaka

Recentring Mother Earth by Andrew Nyongesa

Language, Thought, Art and Existence by Tendai Rinos Mwanaka

Zimbabwe: The Urgency of Now by Tendai Rinos Mwanaka

Experimental Writing, Africa Vs Latin America Vol 1 by Tendai Rinos Mwanaka and Ricardo Felix Rodriguez

Fixing Earth Anthology: An anthology of Africa, UK and Ireland Writers, Vol 2 by Tendai Rinos Mwanaka

https://facebook.com/MwanakaMediaAndPublishing/

www.ingramcontent.com/pod-product-compliance
Lightning Source LLC
Chambersburg PA
CBHW010114270326
41929CB00023B/3352